Poetic Epiphany:
How to Find Peace

Dorian S. Withrow Jr.

Copyright

ISBN

Paperback: 979-8-9900379-5-3

Hardcover: 979-8-9900379-6-0

E-Book: 979-8-9900379-7-7

Publisher: Dorian S. Withrow Jr. / Withrow, LLC

List of Previous Works:

Thoughts of Creativity King 114 Realities

Thoughts Of Creativity King 114 Realities is a creative self-help book. It comprises unique free-verse poetry, illustrations, haikus, and short stories. This book aims to help people cultivate themselves and think about their existence. The goal is to inspire people to make changes within themselves and others around them. Readers contemplate forgiveness, vulnerability, social issues, and goals through free verse poetry. Illustrations bring an authentic and sincere visual aspect to the poetic work. Haikus add flavor to small implementations of imagery and meaning. The author also added short stories. These are personal stories from his life. These stories have moral and ethical lessons to help people overcome their troubles and misconceptions about life. This book took six years to produce. The work in this book comes heavily from experience. The experience comes from his own life and his perception of other people's conditions, actions, and mentalities. Readers will learn from the author and themselves by self-examining and analyzing their reflections on their lives. This book allows people, young and old, to read something relatable. The creative components will develop the reader's cravings for more.

Wisdom 45 Advice

Wisdom 45 Advice is a book with 45 topics that touch on essential subjects such as friendship, communication, vulnerability, money, and more. The topics have an abundance of life lessons and philosophy. This book has helped people take new perspectives and steps to reach their goals. The book has illustrations and poetic elements for creative, friendly readers. Most importantly, this literature is more than just absorbing information; it is a toolbox. As readers embark on their growth journey, they will improve their ability to combat inevitable troubles like grief. You will also understand what it means to learn yourself, how to stay persistent and focused, and how to make a vision come true.

WISDOM 45
ADVICE

Dorian S. Withrow Jr.

Conversations You Need

Conversations You Need is a self-help book made of dialogue and quotes. Engage in honest conversations for moral and ethical education. Learn what it is like to overcome trials and fear. What does it mean to forgive and strengthen a family? How should you approach the steps to meet your goals? How should one deal with grief or criticism? *Conversations You Need* is a fast and easy read, which is excellent for a different approach to learning. This book is perfect for anyone having a busy, sad, great, or lazy day. Anyone can pick up this book to learn and contemplate the conversations needed for self-development.

Don't Be a Cactus:

How to Make Connections & Resolve Conflicts

We need to improve our relationships and maintain our connection to the community. These days, the bonds among people closest to us seem so distant. On other days, our community members feel like they are on their island. Part of what helps us succeed and thrive involves healthy relationships. With a captivating blend of science and practical advice, "Don't Be A Cactus" introduces readers to a fresh perspective on building connections. Don't Be A Cactus dives into what individuals need to do and internalize for themselves to improve their relationships. This new book offers a mirror through which readers can reflect on their relationship dynamics. Many tools assist in understanding what leads people to have good friends, lasting intimate relationships, and make the most of opportunities for their goals. What can you do to improve your connection to others?

DON'T
BE A
~~CACTUS~~

MF, says "I learned a lot about ways to improve my relationships. I have a new way of dealing with people, and I am happy about it."

Dorian S. Withrow Jr.

Withrow LLC

Withrow, LLC is a consulting company that helps people become authors. Its mission is to help people meet their aspirations. Participants will learn what it takes to self-publish their literature. They will gain all the necessary knowledge and resources to make their author goals come to life. Other services include speaking engagements and healing circles. Speaking engagements touch on topics of self-development, growth, and goal setting. Participants will learn what it takes to form goals, meet goals, and transform into a better self. Healing circles allow people to share a comfortable, confidential, and welcoming space for vulnerability, overcoming trauma, growth, and bonding.

Reviews

Reviews play a vital role for both future readers and the author, serving as a bridge between the content and its audience. For future readers, reviews offer honest insights that go beyond marketing blurbs and back cover summaries.

For authors, reviews are invaluable feedback tools. They offer constructive criticism and praise that can inform future writing, identify what resonated most with readers, and sometimes even shape the direction of sequels or future projects. Positive reviews can boost visibility, as many platforms and algorithms elevate highly rated books, while critical reviews—when respectful and specific—can encourage growth and refinement in an author's craft.

A comprehensive review typically includes a summary of the book without spoilers, an evaluation of key elements (plot, content, writing style), and a subjective reaction from the reviewer. It may also comment on originality, emotional resonance, or how well the book fits its genre. The best reviews strike a balance between personal opinion and objective analysis, offering enough context to help others without giving too much away.

In short, reviews are a form of dialogue that benefit the entire literary ecosystem—guiding readers, supporting authors, and fostering community through shared reflections and recommendations.

The Power of Reader Word-of-Mouth

One of the most meaningful ways readers can support a book—beyond purchasing it—is by sharing their honest thoughts with others. Word-of-mouth is powerful. When a reader takes the time to leave a review, post on social media, or recommend a book to a friend, they're doing more than just sharing a good read—they're guiding fellow readers toward a story that might resonate with them too. For other readers, these personal endorsements serve as trusted signposts in a sea of options. A thoughtful review can help someone decide if a book is right for them, and hearing excitement from a fellow reader often carries more weight than any advertisement. For the author, word-of-mouth is invaluable. Reviews and shares increase a book's visibility, boost its credibility, and help it reach wider audiences. For independent and emerging authors especially, this kind of organic support can make a critical difference in a book's success and longevity. When readers speak up, they not only help each other discover meaningful stories—they help ensure those stories continue to be told.

"Put your achievements on display, however honorable or many you have; it does not matter. You achieved it, so let it empower you. Take pride and be proud of what you've accomplished."

Mr. Dorian S. Withrow Jr.

Table of Contents

Contact

Author: Dorian S. Withrow Jr.

Social media: Instagram, Tik Tok, Twitter

- @dorianwithrowjr / Dorian Withrow Jr.

Website

- www.dswjr.com

Email

- withrowauthors@gmail.com

Why Read This Book?

This book is a poetic epiphany—a unique blend of poetry and short essays crafted to inspire creative learning, personal growth, and emotional healing. I wrote it to offer an accessible, engaging journey that empowers anyone to shift their life, find moments of leisure, and improve themselves from within.

The book is divided into two complementary sections:

The Poetry Section

Here, you will find free-verse, introspective poems exploring themes of self-discovery, resilience, and the beauty of the human experience. Each poem invites you to pause and connect deeply with your inner self. Poetry has been a powerful tool for me—helping me release pain, experience catharsis, and achieve self-understanding. It has fueled my personal growth since I discovered it at a young age. My hope is that these poems will offer you the same healing and empowerment.

The Essays Section

In these thoughtful, practical essays, I dive into philosophical and actionable topics around personal development. From mindfulness and self-compassion to embracing change and pursuing your passions, these essays are designed to provide wisdom and tools to transform challenges into opportunities for growth. They address overcoming obstacles like grief, judgment, and bias—barriers that disrupt our peace. Through this prose, you'll gain insights to deepen your understanding of yourself and your place in the world.

Both sections work together to introduce or reinforce teachings that elevate your self-awareness and well-being—because improving yourself ultimately helps those around you.

Why Peace Matters

Peace is a universal yearning, yet it often feels just out of reach. Peace is not simply the absence of conflict or chaos; it is a profound state of calm, balance, and inner harmony. It is the foundation on which we build better relationships, make wiser choices, and lead fulfilling lives. Without peace, our minds become battlegrounds for fear, anger, bias, and regret. With peace, we unlock resilience, clarity, and the capacity to grow—even amid life's toughest challenges.

Peace shapes everything about how we experience the world: our emotions, self-esteem, interactions, and ultimately, our happiness. Without it, we react impulsively, trapped in cycles of judgment and doubt. With it, we reclaim control over our emotional landscape, living authentically, courageously, and purposefully.

Who This Book Is For

This book is born from personal journeys and real-life lessons—a collection of stories, insights, and practical tools designed to help you navigate your emotions, dismantle bias, cultivate self-esteem, and build the poise necessary to thrive. It is for anyone who is overwhelmed by inner struggles or external pressures. It is for those who want more than survival—they want to live intentionally, with peace and strength.

Within these pages, you will discover:

- Why managing emotions is about understanding and growth, not suppression
- How self-esteem is a dynamic journey shaped by your mindset and choices
- How bias steals peace—and how awareness can restore it
- How to take ownership of your emotional well-being and step confidently into your power

Peace is not passive. It is a courageous, deliberate practice that requires honesty, effort, and sometimes boldness. This book invites you to take the first step on that path, equipping you with the wisdom and tools to transform your life from the inside out.

If You Are Ready

If you are ready to break free from noise, judgment, and turmoil; if you want to build a life grounded in calm, confidence, and connection—this book is for you. Together, we will embark on the path to peace, one mindful choice at a time.

Section I: Poetry

Discover the Heart and Journey Within

Prepare to embark on an intimate voyage through the soul's landscape — where raw emotion meets reflection, and personal truth dances with universal experience. This collection of poetry is not just a book; it is a mirror held up to the complexities of life, love, pain, and resilience.

Within these pages, you will find the pulse of human experience — unfiltered and unapologetic. From the quiet moments of self-doubt and the heavy weight of missed chances, to the tender embrace of hope and the fierce determination to grow, each poem invites you to witness the unfolding of a spirit committed to healing and transformation.

You'll walk alongside the poet as they confront the shadows of bias and broken relationships, unravel the knots of internal conflict, and find strength in vulnerability. These verses capture the subtle nuances of everyday struggle: the sting of misunderstood intentions, the tension between pride and humility, and the complex dance of family ties.

Yet, even in the darkest lines, there is a persistent light — a call to embrace empathy, seek connection, and choose peace.

This collection pulses with vivid imagery — from the delicate bloom of a flower struggling to grow, to the endless expanse of the night sky that holds the moon's silent promise. You'll hear the hum of cicadas, feel the warm wind on your skin, and sense the steady rhythm of footsteps walking toward new beginnings. Every poem acts as a stepping stone toward greater self-awareness and communal understanding.

Beyond the personal, these poems address collective experiences — the societal biases that disrupt peace, the challenge of maintaining a positive outlook amid chaos, and the courage it takes to stand firm in one's integrity and values. They remind us that growth is rarely linear, that wounds can become wisdom, and that every day holds the potential for redemption and renewal.

Whether you come to this book seeking comfort in shared struggle, inspiration to face your own battles, or simply the beauty of well-crafted words, you will find a companion here. The poet's voice is both a balm and a beacon — honest and encouraging, sometimes mournful, often hopeful.

As you turn each page, prepare to be challenged and uplifted. These poems ask hard questions, invite deep reflection, and gently urge you to look beyond surface judgments — to find unity in diversity, peace in conflict, and joy even in imperfection.

This is more than poetry. It's a journey through life's storms and sunlight, a testament to human resilience, and an invitation to grow alongside someone who dares to face their truth. Dive in, and let this collection change how you see yourself, others, and the world around you.

We All Must Go

One day, you'll regret the way you've treated
people.
Authority does not give you the right—
Nor does the height of the kite called pride.
One day, you'll wish you had treated people better.
We all make mistakes—*we*, including you and I.

I never understood your hostility;
Often, I questioned your hospitality.
Words can weigh heavy—
You shouldn't take them lightly.

Haiku # 1

Pride flies like a kite—

One day, regret will settle.

Words can weigh like stone.

Why Be Grateful?

I'm grateful for the growth, for the support.
I am grateful for my body.
The sky shines bright, just like her smile—
The smile that brought the sun.

Welcome opportunities and safe spaces;
Both keep family and friends in good health.

Take comfort in blindingly bright days
Amidst adversity and struggle.
Both have their strengths—
Like the cold ocean on a lunar night.

Embrace the days when warm weather brought
comfort.

Haiku # 2

Grateful for the sun,

Warm smiles shine through storms and waves—

Comfort follows light.

Both Progress & Discontent

I ponder whether my work is worth it.

I'm clouded by thoughts of society's standards—

They leave me discouraged, feeling worthless.

I give the best of myself.

The world sees me, yet somehow I remain blind to it.

Still, I'm actively working toward the day

These thoughts become nothing more than a pest.

Haiku # 3

Is my work enough?

Standards cloud what I can't see—

I fight to feel whole.

We Aren't Enemies

I'm on my 97th missed call.
That's an exaggeration—but the 96th felt like a
hundred.
Is it really a missed call when the person saw it and
chose to decline?
They acknowledged it—then dismissed it.

I crawled into my space, laid inclined,
While my emotions hit a steady decline.
After a moment of anger, I sighed—and cried.
I wondered if it was all a lie.

Seventeen years in school,
And I've never searched this long for an answer to a
single question.

Another woman is gone.
Another test I've failed.

After the 99th text and third block, I finally gained
clarity.
I could have been more patient.

I could have been more understanding.
I know I wasn't the best.

I forgot the little things that kept us in love
And replaced them with grudges.
I wanted revenge for other things—
So I didn't show up.

Now, I've been trying to win you back with all my
might.
Applying what I learned in counseling,
Hoping it would work out.

But after seeing all the messages left on read,
I know it didn't.
I even popped up—
Brought edible arrangements, hoping to break down
the wall.

I prayed to God, hoping you would call out.
And no matter how much time has passed,
I still find myself nearly bawling my eyes out.

I wonder if you caught my gaze
As I looked into the cameras during TV

interviews—

It seems to be all I have left of you.

When I stare at the ceiling at night,

I wonder if it was all worth it—

Every time I ignored you,

Dismissed your needs

In pursuit of what I already had in you.

I'd do anything

For you to come back to me.

Haiku # 4

Missed calls fill the air,

Regret sits deep in my chest—

Still, I hope you call.

Trajectory

They will hate you for your trajectory.
What a mess for me, as you flipped through the
pages and engaged your senses.
You found yourself married to jealousy.

When I look up, I see the Great Provider—
The nurturer and life-giver.
But you see a different sun.

I am the moon that blocks out your fruitless
aspiration.
Things changed as I moved into position.
As I kept going, the day grew darker for you.

I need to step out of the way for you to receive your
light.
Over a hundred and sixty-five pages of
consistency—
Still, I am out of reach in this galaxy.

You can bank on this shooting star that won't fall.
This is not an affirmation; it is a promise: wish me

well.

This moon does not move because of you.

Which path should you take?

A man chose peace.

I watched a man get clowned for avoiding a fight,

As the crowd blew balloons and applied makeup.

The pacifist was confused, overwhelmed, and

embarrassed.

"Why fight?"

"What good will come?"

"Who will benefit?"

"Where will it end?"

"How can I end this?"

The pacifist questioned why all these people

laughed

When he refused to fight.

Haiku # 5

Moon blocks your bright light,

Pacifist stands, crowd laughs loud—

Peace outshines the fight.

Birthdate

The date the bud opened,

The day destiny was designed and decided.

Two gardeners, too young to plant by society's
standards.

Through struggle and support, they were able to sort
the cards in hand.

They play well with the deck they were dealt.

In the process of playing the game, they cut their
hands as they shuffled.

There was a lot of stumbling, often biting off more
than they could chew, and the cookie often
crumbled.

With the right environment and gardeners, any
flower can reach its highest height.

Haiku # 6

Bud unfolds its fate,

Young gardeners learn through trials—

Flowers reach sky high.

What Is Delayed Gratification?

Yes, I haven't moved around much, but I am
prepared for a couple of rainy days.
When it pours down, I have an umbrella.
I'm mocked, but when a storm hits you, the jokes
stop.
When something happens to you, it's like everyone
can be fought.
Everyone is grown until they have to regulate
emotions.
They keep it all bottled up until a great explosion—
That used to be me.
I'm not as mad as you, and now you hate me.
We aren't saving the same things.
I'm storing up knowledge and savoring my fortune,
A full-course meal of gratification.

Haiku # 7

Rain falls, I stand calm,

Umbrella shields from the storm—

Silent strength grows deep.

Heaven

Lately, I've been more fascinated with space.

Today, the sky is covered in puffy, cotton

candy–like clouds—

Blends of orange, blue, and purple.

The atmosphere is warm and windy,

A combination that would rock me to sleep.

Have you ever felt that ideal weather condition?

They come once in a while, but not for long.

Haiku # 8

Cotton clouds drift by,

Warm winds blend the twilight hues—

Dreams rock me to sleep.

Two I've Lost

It's not my fault.

I'm blaming you—if not you, then who?

We were distant, and I didn't have a clue about me

and you.

The beautiful woman sang:

"It's your fault.

Did you account for what you did?

Mnm, Mnm, Mnm, Mnm, Mnm, Mnm, Mnm,

Mnm."

I know it's my fault.

Maybe if I had planned better…

I guess I was selfish and lost,

Scared more than anything.

The beautiful woman sang:

"It's no one's fault.

Both of you are still learning.

Don't burn yourself trying to blame anyone.

You have a ways to go.

Mnm, Mnm, Mnmmmmhhmm, Mnm, Mnm,

Mnm."

Is it weird to miss them?

They never came, and I feel like I was the only one to blame.

I hate my attitude and tongue.

The words I can never take back poisoned my opportunity.

I can't help but think what they'd think of me up there.

The beautiful woman sang:

"Mnm, Mnm, Mnmmmm."

Haiku # 9

Blame dances in words,

Learning softens heavy hearts—

Silent songs remain.

No Action Benefits

I was reading a book on Taoism.
I wondered how someone can change so much
without doing much—
The one who brings good fortune to others,
The being whose work often goes unnoticed,
Everything done without reward.

As I've grown, I've noticed that living well and
achieving helps.
By living my destiny, I've inspired others to grow
and change.
I've been influenced to adopt a different way of life
and let go of the old.
It's obvious, yet it's not tied to me.

When you change your ways, others change theirs.

Haiku # 10

Change without action,

Quiet hands shape destinies—

Others follow suit.

Locs & Bars

They'd ask how long I still have to grow.
I replied that I don't know anymore.
I wasn't thinking about lawn care at the time.
Some don't like the look of long grass, but it's the
environment that suits me.

I'm bonded to my goals tighter than the locks in my
hair.
I've been achieving my goals longer than my locs
have grown.
When the grass was low, some laughed.
As the grass grew, some stopped to look as they
passed.

Soon, the onlookers followed suit.
Look at that—now I've got a little community and
crew.
It seemed all they needed was an example.

Haiku # 11

Long grass grows with me,

Eyes once closed now follow close—

Roots bind goals and me.

Through the Fog of Anger

I'm glad my father was around,
At least, he was present.
At most, it seemed he worked,
But not everything worked out.

There were bumps in the road, of course,
But who hasn't tripped, slipped, or fallen down?

Through the good, the neutral, the bad, and the
beautiful,
I wouldn't be in the position I'm in now.

Like a Taoist, I see life taking its own course.
As hard as we try, we don't control where it goes or
how things unfold—
At least, it seems this way.

Although that doesn't mean we shouldn't try
To live the way we want.

Through the ugly, the bad, the neutral, and the good,
I'm grateful for him.

We don't make the best decisions,

But I'm thankful for him.

Haiku # 12

Glad my father stayed,

Life's course winds beyond control,

Grateful through it all.

How Does It Go Again?

I'm content with life—
I mean the way it has been, the way it is.
It's made up of the cards dealt and the choices we
make.
That's what I remind myself in front of the person
Screwing up their face and scrutinizing.

I chose something different—what about you?
There are an astounding number of people worse off
than both of us.
Somehow I'm the problem because of your
inadequacies.

What I've learned is it's never too late.
What I've done is change my ways.
What I do is change others, with whatever I can
muster.

Don't get me wrong—I have my own faults too.
Yeah, I have fallen short a few times.
As I write this, for goodness' sake, I shouldn't be
eating two scoops of bubblegum ice cream.

For the sake of health, I knew I shouldn't have stayed up late.

But nothing was keeping me up except my own choice.
Just like nothing should keep you down—inside or outside of your choices.

Haiku # 13

Life's dealt cards and choice,

We rise despite flaws and faults,

Freedom lies within.

What Life Will Bring

I'm excited for what's to come for me.

My interaction with bees yesterday was pretty comforting.

I get to see the flowers bloom and hear the birds chirp soon.

A clear, bright sky keeps me grounded.

Even at times when I am flying through the clouds, it's hard to find many things to keep me down.

I look forward to seeing the answers assembled to feed their queen,

Or the cats and snakes sunbathing.

I love seeing the trees grow their leaves back.

The waves on a warm, windy day make worries go away,

That same feeling when the dogs come out to play,

And when the cicadas sing away.

When times are tough, it is better to think about the good in today and even the things that seem far away.

Haiku # 14

Bees hum, flowers bloom,

Waves and leaves dance with the breeze—

Hope in every day.

A.H. & J.B.

I haven't found the perfect way to start this poem.
It's been a long time since I've talked to you two—
How long has it been?
Weeks, months, maybe years?

From the very start, you both showed a different
kind of heart—
One that didn't need a push to begin.
Before you both left, I don't know if you knew,
But you made a mark—
A mark on me.

Among the few people I've met in my lifetime,
I can confidently say I admire both of you.
Before we argue over who admires whom more,
Let me finish this thought.

Among all the congratulations and compliments,
It meant the most coming from you.
My only regret is that I didn't give it back—
Not equally, and certainly not enough.

I think I speak for many when I say this:
Sometimes happiness feels like the missing piece in
my life—
That kind of happiness you both naturally exude.

There were smiles every time we came together,
Laughs and jokes every time we parted—
That's what I remember most.

I have no memory of trying to help you both.
I didn't know what you were going through—
I suppose that's part of life.

I write this with a smile, repeating aloud:
"You remember the advice you asked for,
Randomly calling me about breathing and
meditation."
I remember your excitement trying new things.

And you—
"You remember when you tripped and fell after that
jump shot?"
I remember you making fun of mistakes like a
champion.

It's been some time, but your absence still hurts.
I hope putting this poem down now helps keep the
memories alive.

You were both free spirits with your own paths.
I wish I could go back and give you all I had,
So this poem wouldn't need to be written.

You would tell me to live my life,
To embrace the future you were excited to see me
build.
And after we read this together,
You'd tell me how much you want to be like me—

But neither of you realize,
I've always wanted to be like you.

I know some of the pain came from those who
wouldn't listen.
Telling you to carry on, to suck it up, without care.
And there were those who simply didn't care at
all—
A little lacking in humanity.

Yet, there were those who cared, who lent a hand—
And to them, I owe my commitment to this journey.

I'm saying "I do!" every day—
Involuntarily, like an "achoo."

I love you, brothers.

Haiku # 14

Brothers gone away,

Memories like whispered wind—

Love remains, steadfast.

Section II: Lessons

Wounds to Wisdom

This section explores the deeply human experiences we often carry in silence—grief, bias, conflict, self-perception, judgment, and unresolved pain. These essays are a tapestry of reflection and reality, woven from personal stories, spiritual grounding, and emotional truth. Each piece offers an invitation: not only to witness pain, but to transform it into peace, purpose, and clarity.

We begin with loss—the emotional terrain of grief. Here, death is not seen as an end, but a transformation. Drawing from African spiritual traditions and personal family experiences, we explore how language, memory, and culture shape the way we mourn and heal. This opening essay reminds us that grief is not linear—it is layered, and it changes us. But through tools like writing, martial arts, spirituality, and service, we can process sorrow and rediscover stillness within ourselves.

From grief, we move into reflection on life's urgency. What would you do if you had only 30 days left to live? Through this lens, we explore legacy, family, dreams, and the desire to impact future generations. It's a reminder that urgency can birth clarity—and clarity can realign our priorities toward what truly matters.

As the section progresses, we navigate bias—not just in society, but in how it enters homes and hospital rooms, shaping experiences and outcomes. Through powerful real-life examples, these essays confront the impact of racial and cultural bias, particularly in healthcare, and call for deeper awareness and responsibility.

But personal growth isn't only born from hardship. It's also nurtured through passion. The essay on martial arts and creative expression illustrates how consistent engagement in hobbies—whether painting, walking, or Taekwon-do—can improve discipline, heal stress, and deepen self-respect. The environments we cultivate, both physically and emotionally, have the power to restore us.

Conflict, a recurring theme in this section, is presented not as something to fear, but something to face. We learn how unresolved conflict can harden perspectives and create mental and emotional distance from others. Yet, through honest reflection, forgiveness, boundaries, and proactive healing, we reclaim the ability to trust and connect again.

The common thread through all of these essays is this: peace is not the absence of problems—it is the presence of understanding. It is the result of self-inquiry, humility, and continuous effort to see life clearly and respond with intention.

This section is for anyone carrying something heavy. For those trying to forgive what hurt them, to make peace with the past, to find clarity in their values, or to redefine their identity in the face of trials. These pages offer not just stories, but soul work. They invite readers to reflect, reframe, and move forward—heart, awareness, and a deepened sense of self.

Reputation

These thoughts aren't in any particular order—but they carry weight.

Reputation is one of the most interesting and powerful forces in human interaction. It shapes how the world treats you—and, just as importantly, how you treat the world in return. It can be armor against negativity or a magnet for it. It can open doors or close them. At its best, reputation is quiet security. At its worst, it becomes a shadow that follows your every move.

We live in a time where visibility is higher than ever. Social media, digital portfolios, and online impressions are part of daily life for people young and old. As a result, we must be **more conscious than ever** of how we're perceived—and why that perception matters.

What Makes a "Good" Reputation?

A good reputation is not about popularity. It's not about fame or optics. At its core, a good reputation is about **character**—about the alignment between actions, words, and values.

It's about who you are when no one's watching, and whether your positive qualities shine stronger than your flaws behind closed doors. It's about how you treat people and how you contribute to the environment.

A good reputation comes from consistency, respect, and benefit:

- **Consistency** in your words and actions
- **Respect** for others, regardless of their status
- **Benefit** to those around you—whether through your skills, service, or presence

That might mean giving back through your art, martial arts, culinary skills, financial knowledge, or technology. It could mean showing up for your community in small but meaningful ways. In my case, it comes through my **work in media and literature**—sharing messages that uplift, educate, and offer perspective.

Let Your Work Speak

The people around you ultimately decide your reputation. You don't control their thoughts—but you **do control your effort, your integrity, and the quality of what you put into the world**. Let your work speak for itself.

Your reputation is tied to the **results you produce**, yes—but also to the **relationships you maintain**. If you've left a trail of broken connections, mistrust, or manipulation, it's only a matter of time before your reputation reflects that. Conversely, if people speak well of you when you're not in the room—that's a sign you're building something real.

A good reputation can bring:

- **Opportunities** (job offers, partnerships, invitations)
- **Loyalty** from peers and collaborators
- **Protection** from people with ill intent—because others will step in on your behalf

In many ways, a solid reputation becomes your **social insurance**. People are less likely to spread rumors, treat you with malice, or disrespect you publicly when your name is known to stand for something good.

The Other Side: A Bad Reputation

Bad reputations, on the other hand, often stem from repeated harm. They grow from patterns—of crime, cruelty, dishonesty, manipulation, or selfishness. A negative reputation can lead to:

- **Isolation**

- **Disrespect**
- **Limited opportunities**
- **Distrust—even when change is attempted**

There are, of course, exceptions. Some people with bad reputations are treated well due to status or fear. And some people with great reputations are mistreated due to envy or bias. But overall, **a good reputation garners more allies, more protection, and more peace of mind.**

People are more likely to **follow the lead of a good reputation**. They'll align with it. Defend it. Amplify it. That energy creates momentum—and that momentum leads to a higher quality of life.

Final Thought: Reputation Is Legacy in Motion

Think of your reputation as **a living legacy**. It's what people carry with them after your name leaves their lips. And it's not built in a day. It's shaped through the choices you make—**how you show up, who you serve, and what you stand for.**

Let the quality of your work, your relationships, and your values speak so clearly that your name becomes **a signal of trust**—not just success.

Because when your reputation aligns with your true character, you won't have to constantly prove who you are.

You'll already be known.

Problem of Judgment: Jewelry Story

I want to share one of many personal experiences that fuels my commitment to both personal and professional growth. It's a story that reminds me just how powerful—and damaging—prejudgment can be.

Judgment, when rooted in fear or assumption, becomes a silent plague. It doesn't always shout, but it divides. It limits. It reinforces false narratives. Yes, we all make judgments to some degree. The real difference lies in what we choose to do with them. Growth begins the moment we stop letting those judgments guide our actions—and instead learn to see people with clarity, not inference.

The Moment

As part of the **Breaking Barriers** program, I was selected—alongside a few other young men—to attend a gun violence prevention conference in

Baltimore. On our second day in the city, we had some free time to explore and found ourselves wandering into a massive shopping mall.

We eventually stepped into a jewelry store—four young African American men, wide-eyed and curious. The sparkle of the diamonds pulled us in like doves released from a cage at a wedding. In that moment, we were married to beauty.

We spread out across the showroom floor, admiring the brilliance behind the glass:

- "Is it really worth that much?"
- "I'm going to have to save up for that!"
- "Darn—$9,000?"

We laughed, we asked questions, we admired the stones. But behind the counter, something shifted.

Three employees grew tense. Hyper-vigilant. One wore an unmistakably hardened expression. Suspicion thickened the air. It wasn't hard to guess what they were thinking.

The Shift

That's when our program director stepped in. Calmly, warmly, he struck up a conversation with the staff.

"These young men are part of Breaking Barriers," he explained. "He just finished college and published a book. These two are pursuing their master's degrees in media arts and education. And he's finishing high school while creating original music."

It was like flipping a switch.

Another staff member joined in, and slowly, the energy in the room changed. The tension began to melt. The suspicion softened. And then, something beautiful happened.

One of the jewelers invited us to sit down. What followed was an impromptu **20-minute crash course on diamonds**—cut, clarity, color, carat. We learned about the microscopic differences that define value. We were taught how to tell a real diamond from a fake one—sometimes with the naked eye.

This wasn't just window-shopping anymore. It became a full-on education.

The jeweler handed me his card and said, "When you're ready to get engaged, call me." He even explained how we could become certified in diamond evaluation and jewelry making if we ever wanted to.

The Deeper Truth

But here's the truth: **none of that would have happened if we weren't given a chance**—if we hadn't been seen for who we really were.

Without that shift in perspective, we might have walked away with nothing but another quiet, painful memory of being misunderstood. Just four young

Black men "lingering" in a jewelry store—brushed off, judged, unseen.

Instead, we left with knowledge, connection, and empowerment.

Why This Matters

This story is one of many that continues to shape my belief in how **experience can transform perception**. It's a reminder that when we take the time to look past assumptions and bias, we don't just avoid harm—we open doors. We share wisdom. We build bridges that wouldn't exist otherwise.

Moments like this don't just happen. They are created—through presence, through advocacy, through someone being willing to say, "See them for who they are."

The Mission

This is why I strive to grow—not just for myself, but to reshape how we treat one another. To challenge the assumptions we too often make. To create space for others to be seen, heard, and respected.

Because **one conversation can change the atmosphere**. One open heart can turn suspicion into mentorship. And one shared experience can stay with someone for a lifetime.

Let's do more than break barriers. Let's replace them—with understanding, opportunity, and truth.

Problem of Bias

Bias is more than just a flawed perception—it's a
disruptor of peace. It doesn't simply distort how we
see others; it damages lives, relationships, and trust.
It unsettles not only the people it targets but also
those who witness and carry it. I know this not just
as a social truth, but as a personal reality—through
the story of my mother.

It began on what was supposed to be a joyful day: a
family birthday celebration at a trampoline park.
The energy was high, the laughter abundant. Then,
in one swift moment, joy turned to tragedy. While
jumping, my mother tore something in her right
knee. What followed was a surgery meant to
heal—but instead, it changed her life forever.

When Pain Is Dismissed

After the operation, during her post-op recovery, my
mother was in unbearable pain. Initially, her pain

was acknowledged. She was given medication. But it wasn't enough—and worse, that compassion didn't last.

Her voice—the pain in it—began to be questioned. She felt it immediately: they didn't believe her. Maybe they thought she was exaggerating. Maybe they suspected drug seeking. Whatever it was, the compassion faded into cold skepticism. Despite clear, visible signs of suffering—swelling, tears, immobility—her cries were minimized. She was told the pain would pass. But it didn't.

She returned home—to me, my younger brother, and my aunt. We were just kids. But we knew something was deeply wrong. Her agony was constant, sharp, and raw. No position brought relief. No remedy worked. We were scared. Confused. Powerless.

Eventually, desperate, she returned to the hospital. That's when the truth came out: during the original procedure, the surgeon had accidentally severed an artery behind her knee, causing internal bleeding.

She had also sustained permanent nerve damage. A second surgery was needed to repair the damage—but by then, it was too late. The injury had already altered her life.

When Bias Becomes a Barrier to Care

After that, everything changed in our household. My father was away for years, so as the eldest, I had to step up. I became her caregiver, the emotional support for my siblings, and a child forced into an adult world. It was a crash course in growing up. But more than that, it was my first intimate encounter with **systemic bias**.

My mother is a Black woman—and Black women, far too often, are not believed when they express pain. There is a long-standing, deeply harmful stereotype that Black women are inherently stronger, more pain tolerant, or emotionally dramatic. These myths are rooted in racism and misogyny—and they continue to infect healthcare today.

Bias nearly cost my mother her life.

This wasn't just a medical error. It was a failure to *listen*. A failure to *care*. A failure of humanity wrapped in professional uniforms and polite condescension.

Bias Is Not Just a Social Issue—It's a Peace Issue

That's why we must actively confront bias—not just in institutions, but in ourselves. Because bias is more than prejudice-it's a peace thief. It robs individuals of dignity. It reshapes families. It hijacks futures. It changes how people live, parent, work, and heal.

Bias in healthcare kills.

Bias in schools holds kids back.

Bias in workplaces limits potential.

Bias in daily interactions chips away at someone's self-worth and security—often without the person holding the bias even noticing.

We cannot afford to treat this lightly.

The Call to Confront It

We owe it to each other to name bias when we see it. To question it when it appears in conversations, decisions, or silence. To uproot it from systems that pretend to serve everyone equally. To ensure that no one's pain is ignored again—especially due to the color of their skin, their gender, or the story someone else tells about them before they speak for themselves.

Bias isn't just a civil rights issue. It's a peace issue. And peace—real, deep, sustaining peace—can't exist where bias is allowed to thrive.

Let us not wait for someone we love to suffer before we start paying attention. Let us challenge bias *now*, so that one day, fewer people have to tell stories like mine.

Peace at Home:
What Keeps Stress Away?

Activities outside of work and school make all the difference in shaping a peaceful, balanced life. Yet, so many people haven't discovered that *thing*—that spark, that joy, that reason to stay up a little later or wake up a little earlier. If you haven't found something that brings enthusiasm into your day, I hope my story helps you recognize a path to get there.

I've met artists who create breathtaking portraits, expressing their emotions through brushstrokes and swirls of color. I've encountered musicians who breathe life into drums, strings, and harmonies—offering soundtracks for healing. I've seen dancers reveal the complexities of the human body in motion, storytelling through rhythm and space. All of them, in their own way, found a passion that gives their days meaning.

For me, one of those passions is **martial arts**. It's not just something I do—it's something that *does*

something to me. It grounds me, sharpens me, and
opens doors I never knew existed.

My Journey into Taekwon-Do

I practice ITF Taekwon-do, a Korean martial art,
and I've been in love with it for over five years. I
currently hold the rank of *Ee Dan*—a second degree
Black Belt. But the journey began much earlier,
long before belts or ranks meant anything to me.

It started with my grandfather. He used to take my
brother and me to parks and waterfronts, teaching
us the basics—kicks, punches, stances. We shared
laughs, soaked in the summer sun, and ended our
sessions with ice cream. I still remember the blue,
pink, and purple bubblegum flavors melting over
my fingers as if I were in a race against the heat.

Eventually, life shifted. Time became scarce, and
we stopped meeting. I enrolled in college and found
a job. But something in me still craved the structure,

the challenge, the discipline. So I took initiative. I found the Taekwon-do school I now call home.

A Space Designed for Growth

From the moment I walked into the dojang, I could feel the difference. The floor beneath my bare feet had texture—black grooves designed to support movement. There was a sense of order: shoe racks by the door, diffusers releasing peppermint into the air, a quiet hum from a water fountain. Even the air felt intentional.

Every detail in that space existed to support growth—whether it was the padded flooring to protect our joints, the square outlines to give us room to train, or the flags and trophies honoring lineage and legacy.

Before entering the training floor, I was taught to bow—an act of respect not just for the space, but for the growth that takes place within it. That simple

gesture reframed how I approached my
environment. Respect transforms how we treat the
spaces we inhabit—and ourselves.

That idea extends far beyond martial arts. Just like
the dojang, our homes can be places of clarity and
comfort. Spaces can be organized to encourage rest,
creativity, or productivity. We can decorate our
environments with symbols of pride and
achievement—not for vanity, but for
empowerment—making them *monuments of
progress.* Because when we honor our space, we
honor our process.

Leave the Dirt at the Door

One of my favorite rituals in the dojang is leaving
our shoes at the door. Not just for cleanliness, but
for symbolism. Our shoes carry the dust, debris, and
energy of the outside world. When we take them
off, we leave that chaos behind.

It's a reminder that we don't need to carry the weight of the world into every sacred space we enter—be it our home, our creative space, or even a conversation. The same applies to emotional clutter: politics, negativity, bad vibes. Leave them at the "shoe rack."

It's a lesson in mindfulness—and peace.

More Than Just Kicks and Punches

Since joining the dojang, I've formed real connections. I met a fashion designer there, and together we collaborated on a project for my filmmaking class. That partnership turned into a friendship. My passion for martial arts became a gateway to other opportunities—professionally, socially, and personally.

Sometimes, I walk to training. People see me and offer rides. But walking itself is healing. It connects me to my body, to nature, to the present moment. I feel the wind, the sun, and sometimes even the rain—though I keep an umbrella nearby. On those walks, I notice everything: dogs chasing each other, leaves dancing in the breeze, and the stillness of a moment not yet touched by time. It's all therapeutic.

Taekwon-do offers that same presence. When I train, I'm not thinking about yesterday's mistakes or tomorrow's stress. I'm focused—*here and now.* That mindfulness brings peace.

Discovery Through Practice

We often don't know what we're capable of until we begin something new. My martial arts journey has taught me just how much power, speed, and grace I can generate. I've developed spinning kicks, improved flexibility, and found a strength I didn't know I had.

Recently, I also took a painting class for my birthday. I didn't sip—I painted. I was nervous at first, worried I'd mess it up. But with encouragement from the instructors, I followed the steps, trusted the process, and saw something beautiful take shape. My piece didn't look like anyone else's—but that's exactly why it was special. It was uniquely *mine*. I couldn't always see the masterpiece I was creating—but by the end, I saw it clearly.

That's true for all of us. Sometimes, we don't see the growth while we're in it. But that doesn't mean it's not happening.

A Final Thought: Find What Moves You

Whether it's martial arts, painting, writing, music, gardening, or dance, find *your thing*—that activity that brings you peace, that brings you closer to yourself. It doesn't have to be perfect. It just has to be yours.

Let it teach you. Let it center you. Let it become the doorway to discovery—of self, of peace, of purpose.

And once you find it, protect it. Like the dojang, create your space with intention. Fill it with reminders of who you are and what you've accomplished. Respect it. Use it to grow.

Because outside of work and school, there's a whole world waiting to show you what's possible—if you're willing to take the first step.

30 Days Left

I was once asked a question that stopped me in my tracks:

"If you had 30 days left to live, what would you want to do, accomplish, and leave behind?"

It's a question that forces clarity—stripping away distraction and revealing what truly matters. In a world full of noise, reflecting on our final days can bring a deep sense of insight, urgency, and empowerment. But it's not enough to simply *think* about our answers. The power lies in turning those thoughts into *action*.

So, I want to pass that question on to you.
If you had 30 days left, what would you focus on? Who would you reach out to? What would you create, heal, or celebrate before your time was up?

Here's my answer.

What I Want to Leave Behind

At the heart of it all, I want to generate enough
wealth for my family to *thrive*—not just survive.
Everyone has their own definition of what that
looks like. But I've seen firsthand how many of the
hardships people face could be avoided if they had
more access, more resources, more support.

So many of our deepest struggles—whether it's the
food we eat, the stress we carry, the medical
conditions we endure, or the environments we're
raised in—can be traced back to economics. I want
to help break that cycle. I don't just want to hand
people money. I want to teach people how to build
for themselves, especially in communities where
self-sufficiency has been stifled or stolen.

Knowledge is power—but only if it's shared.

I want to break down what I've learned for my
family, my community, and future generations. I

want to leave behind a blueprint—something
tangible that empowers people to build lives rooted
in purpose, wellness, and connection.

The Experiences I Still Want

Beyond family and community, I still have dreams
of exploration and wonder. I've always wanted to
visit islands—to stand barefoot on beaches, soaking
in views that make you stop and just *breathe*. I'm a
visual person. Nature speaks to me. I find peace in
watching animals simply exist in their habitat.
There's something spiritual about it.

Africa calls to me, not just as a destination, but as a
return—to my heritage, to deeper spiritual
understanding, to the food, the language, the rhythm
of the people. I want to immerse myself in it. I want
to taste dishes with unfamiliar names and familiar
souls. Food is, after all, a universal language.

In fact, I recently tried squid for the first time. It reminded me that broadening my horizons doesn't always mean going far—it just means being open.

The Skills I Still Hope to Learn

If I had 30 days left, I'd still want to *train*. I'd spend more time on the mat. I currently practice ITF Taekwon-do—a Korean martial art—and hold a Second-degree black belt. But there's more I want to learn. I've become increasingly interested in throwing arts like Judo. My great-grandmother practiced it. My grandfather was a Karate practitioner. Martial arts runs through my bloodline—and it's one of the ways I stay grounded, focused, and disciplined.

I'd also love to explore cooking—not just as a chore, but as an art. One day, I hope to write about it, maybe even publish something on the subject. There's something beautiful about creating a meal that brings people together.

The Legacy I Hope to Build

I want to own land—not just for status or luxury, but for community. I dream of creating centralized spaces where young people can grow, learn, and thrive. I want hubs where people can organize, collaborate, and build something greater than themselves.

More than anything, I want more *time with my family*. No one in particular—just *everyone*. The joy that comes from being in the same space, laughing, eating, and creating memories . . . that's sacred to me. I want to foster peace and resolution among them. If there's tension or old wounds, I want to help dissolve them. Unity matters.

I want to spend part of my 30 days *teaching the little ones*. Passing down wisdom, stories, and skills the way my great-grandmother did for me. She helped raise me with strength, patience, and deep

love. I want to do the same for the next
generation—so her spirit lives on through me.

The Father I Hope to Be

I don't have children yet—but if I did, I'd want to
give them everything I didn't receive. Not just
material things, but emotional safety, patience,
guidance, and presence. I want to be the kind of
father who shows up with *consistency*, not just
intention.

The Healing I Hope to Begin

Before I go, I want to say *I'm sorry*—to anyone I've
harmed, knowingly or unknowingly. To anyone I
hurt with my ignorance, my ego, or my silence. Life
moves fast, and we don't always realize the wounds
we leave behind. I strive to grow, to evolve, and to
help others do the same.

I want to burn through the negative parts of myself—to cleanse what no longer serves me, and to facilitate healing within my family. If I had 30 days, I'd use them to bridge gaps, open hearts, and remove the barriers to unity. I'd ask others to do the same.

What I Hope You Take from This

This exercise isn't just about imagining your death. It's about *clarifying your life*. The things we'd focus on in our final days are often the things that matter most right now.
So ask yourself again:

If you had 30 days left to live…
What would you do?
What would you say?
What would you leave behind?

Live in alignment with that answer.

Every day.

Until your legacy is no longer a dream—it's
something already unfolding.

Hard Losses

Death is inevitable—and often life-altering. Finding peace after loss, whether sudden or expected, is one of the most difficult emotional journeys we face. My experience with grief, shaped by culture, faith, and personal loss, is not a blueprint, but a mirror—offered in the hope that others might find their own path reflected in mine.

A Spiritual Framework for Grief

I come from an African spiritual background layered with a light Christian upbringing. In many metaphysical African traditions, life is not seen as ending with death. Instead, life transforms. We are spirit first. When we are born, we take on a physical form. And when someone passes, they do not "die"—they *transition*. They return to the spirit world, where they remain conscious, connected, and protective.

This belief has anchored me in my most difficult moments. It reframes death not as erasure, but as continuation. And that framing shaped how I processed the first loss I ever witnessed.

My First Encounter with Death

My great-grandfather was the first person I lost. I wasn't close to him—I knew him through stories more than presence—so when he transitioned, I felt numb. While others mourned with visible emotion, I couldn't access that same depth of feeling.

This is often the case when we lose someone with whom we lacked emotional intimacy. Yet even then, I noticed how the *language* used around death shaped our experience of it. Saying someone "transitioned" rather than "died" softened the finality and opened a door to acceptance. My great-grandmother, his wife, always spoke of him in neutral or gently positive terms—not to glorify him, but to offer peace.

That tone mattered. It showed me how remembering someone in a balanced way helps foster healing. It may have contributed to my numbness—but it also shaped how I'd later carry memory with intention.

A Loss That Hit Closer to Home

Years later, my great-grandmother—the same woman who had taught me how to speak of the dead with grace—began her own transition. She had breast cancer. Over time, I experienced what's known as *anticipatory grief*—mourning someone slowly while they are still physically present. Each visit left tears in my eyes—sometimes during, sometimes afterward. Watching someone you love slowly fade is its own unique pain.

Even now, four years later, I cry writing this. She was strong, wise, full of love, and endlessly encouraging. As a child, I sometimes avoided visiting her—not out of indifference, but because I didn't know how to face the truth. As I grew older, I wanted nothing more than for her to stay.

On her final day, the sorrow was unbearable. Her body had changed. Her speech was gone. And due to the COVID-19 pandemic, I couldn't even hold her hand. Still, I talked to her for the 10–15 minutes I had. I updated her on my life. I told her I loved her. I made peace with what was coming. She tried to respond—mumbling words I couldn't quite catch—but I believe she heard me.

A Tangled Web of Emotions

After the funeral, I felt everything. Anger—that someone so good had to suffer. Guilt—that I hadn't visited more. Shame—that I couldn't afford to help with her care. But also pride—pride that she had seen my growth, that her teachings live through me, and that I can pass those teachings on.

I often remind myself that she's still here, watching. That she hasn't died, not truly. She lives in memory, in story, in spirit. My mother keeps her alive in conversation. And I carry her with me in how I live.

The Grief I Never Spoke About

I never saw a counselor for my grief. Maybe I should have. Maybe I still should. Grief is complicated and ever evolving. Anticipatory grief gave me time to prepare—but it also stretched the suffering over months and years. It was a slow burn, rather than a sudden fire.

Both are hard in different ways. Sudden loss brings shock, leaving us breathless. Anticipatory loss gives us time—but also emotional exhaustion.

Grief shows up in every part of us:

– **Physically** in sleepless nights, lost appetites, and tension in the body.

– **Emotionally** in numbness, anger, guilt, sadness, and even relief.

– **Spiritually** in shaken beliefs, or in faith rediscovered.

– **Behaviorally** in avoidance, distraction, withdrawal, or obsession.

People cope in different ways. Some carry keepsakes. Some avoid places that stir memories. Others seek these same places out for comfort. The depth of grief often reflects the depth of the bond—and how secure or unresolved it felt.

Finding Healing through Movement and Meaning

For me, what helped was remembering the *good*. Honoring the joyful memories. Leaning into practices that brought me peace—like martial arts, which grounded me. And writing, which became my therapy.

Writing gave me space to reflect, release, and reshape the pain. It was both a mirror and a tool—a way to transform sorrow into meaning.

Grief Is Not a Straight Line

Grief doesn't follow a timeline. There is no "getting over it." There is only learning to *carry it differently*. In our fast-paced world, we're quick to distract ourselves from pain, obsessed with chasing happiness. But sometimes, the path to peace starts by sitting with sorrow.

Ask yourself:

– What am I feeling?

– Why?

– Where is this coming from?

Let it flow. Let it speak. But don't let it consume you.

And when it gets too heavy, return to your *medicine*. That may be prayer, therapy, writing, movement, or simply the loving presence of others.

We cannot avoid grief. But we *can* shape how we hold it. In doing so, we honor those we've lost—and we give ourselves permission to grow, to turn sorrow into something sacred, to carry pain with grace, and let it deepen the love we give moving forward.

When Grief Is Not Addressed

What happens when people don't take the time to face what's troubling them? This is my personal reflection on what I believe is necessary to process grief. These are not universal truths—because grief is far too complex and personal for any single approach to fit everyone. Cultural background, age, past experiences, and personal values all shape how we grieve.

Still, I hope that by sharing these thoughts, someone may find a sense of resonance—and perhaps, a little relief.

The Barriers to Grieving

There are many reasons people avoid addressing their grief—some internal, others external. One important concept that often goes unacknowledged is **disenfranchised grief**: the kind of grief people feel they're not allowed to express. This might be because society, family, or cultural norms tell them their grief is illegitimate—or they've internalized that belief themselves.

Sometimes the block is emotional. People raised on the belief that strength means silence—"Don't cry, Toughen up, Don't show weakness"—struggle to allow themselves to feel. In these environments, tears are seen as failure rather than evidence of love.

Other times, people avoid grief because the relationship with the deceased was complicated, unresolved, or painful. There may have been arguments, unspoken regrets, family secrets, or even trauma. Some mourn people they loved but never reconciled with. Others grieve individuals who caused them harm. In these cases, grief becomes tangled in **confusion, guilt, shame, or silence**.

Whether someone is denied the right to grieve by others or denies it to themselves, the result is the same: the pain lingers—unspoken, unprocessed, and unresolved.

The Path Forward: Acknowledgment and Action

So how do we move forward?

Grief begins with **acknowledgment**. We must accept—however painful—that someone is gone. We must be willing to sit with the suffering, to feel it fully, and to move through it at our own pace. Because grief that is buried or ignored doesn't disappear—it festers. Unhealed grief can resurface as anger, anxiety, guilt, depression, or even physical illness. It may echo through our lives years later, triggered by places, smells, anniversaries, or words.

The only way out is through.

And for many, that journey may never truly end. Grief may come in **waves, seasons, or milestones**. It may soften or evolve, but not follow a neat timeline—and that's okay. The point is not to "get over" grief, but to learn how to live with it.

The Tools That Helped Me

I've found certain practices that have helped me along the way.

One of the most vital things has been my practice of **martial arts**. It wasn't just a discipline or a form of exercise—it was a physical release, a grounding force, a way to tend to my body during times of emotional turmoil. Taking care of our physical health, especially when paired with something that brings joy or focus, can be a powerful companion in grief.

Another essential outlet has been **art**. Art is more than self-expression—it is a sacred language beyond words. Through creativity, we can reconnect with the people we've lost, explore our emotions, and better understand ourselves. Whether it's painting, music, dance, or movement, creating something helps make the invisible visible. It becomes a bridge between the seen and unseen, between memory and presence.

Art also helps with **disenfranchised grief**. When no one else acknowledges your loss, your art becomes the witness. It says: *This mattered. This person mattered. My pain matters.*

For me, that outlet was **poetry**. Through it, I released emotions that had no other place to go. I gave form to foggy thoughts. I turned sorrow into rhythm. Poetry became both a mirror and a release—offering clarity, relief, and insight into where I was in my grief.

Grief Is Not a Problem to Solve

In the end, grief is not something to be solved. It is something to be **held, explored, and lived with**. Over time, it may shift in shape or intensity—but it will never be as linear or predictable as we hope.

And that's okay.

What matters most is that we **find our own tools**, find our own rhythm, and above all, give ourselves **permission to grieve**—in whatever way we need.

Addressing Grief with Youth

When children encounter grief, their first response often comes in the form of questions:

- "When is so-and-so coming back?"
- "Where did they go?"
- "Are they in heaven or hell?"
- "Can I still see them?"

These aren't just innocent curiosities—they're attempts to make sense of something vast, unfamiliar, and often frightening. For adults, the most important rule to follow in these moments is simple: **be considerate with your words.** Let the child guide the conversation as much as possible. Allow them to speak, to wonder, and to process in their own time and their own way.

If the child is a relative or someone close to you, you may be able to offer more direct and honest answers. But with children of acquaintances or in professional settings, it's important to proceed with greater caution—especially if you're unsure what the child's guardians have already explained.

Meeting Children Where They Are

Young children often need to be reminded repeatedly about what has happened. Their understanding of death is still forming, and they may not grasp its permanence. Older children, on the other hand, tend to internalize grief more fully—but each child is different. Some will need extra emotional support. Others may retreat into themselves, appearing composed while still needing reassurance and presence from trusted adults.

When I took a class on grief, we spent a portion of it focusing on how to support children who are mourning. One of the most powerful examples came from an unexpected source: **an episode of *Sesame Street*** where Elmo loses his uncle Jack.

In the episode, Elmo struggles to comprehend the reality of the loss. At a family reunion, he continues to bring up Uncle Jack, not realizing he won't be attending. Elmo's cousin Jesse, who is a bit older, reacts differently—she avoids talking about her father altogether. These two responses—**confusion and avoidance**—are among the most common ways children cope with grief.

Later in the episode, Elmo's father gently encourages Jesse to open up. She does—and admits that sharing her feelings helps. Elmo finds comfort in Uncle Jack's belongings. These small, meaningful objects become emotional anchors, providing a tangible connection to someone who's gone.

The adults in the episode model grief in thoughtful, age-appropriate ways. They acknowledge sadness, share memories, and answer questions with care. In one poignant scene, a character named Jill tells a funny story about a prank Uncle Jack once pulled. It reminds viewers that laughter, when grounded in love, can coexist with sorrow—and that storytelling can help children grieve without becoming consumed by the weight of loss.

Another subtle but important moment happens when Elmo's father, trying and failing to open a jar, shows a glimpse of physical weakness. It's a gentle reminder that grief manifests not only emotionally but physically. Later, he invites Jesse to a baseball game—one of Jack's favorite activities—demonstrating how **shared experiences can become rituals of remembrance and healing**.

Adolescents and Grief: A More Complex Terrain

For teenagers, grief becomes even more layered. Adolescence is already a time of emotional turbulence and identity formation. Add the profound disruption of losing someone close, and the emotional intensity can become overwhelming.

Teen grief often feels isolating—especially if peers haven't experienced personal loss themselves. Yet many teens develop **protective and healing outlets**, such as:

- Listening to music
- Journaling or creative writing

- Making art
- Talking with trusted adults or mentors
- Attending grief support groups
- Reflecting quietly on memories of the person they lost

These are healthy responses. Just as important is helping teens recognize that **grief takes time**—and that it may look different for everyone.

One often overlooked factor in teen grief is the **role of schools**. Many educators are not trained to recognize grief in students or understand how it shows up. A grieving student might act out, withdraw, or lose focus—not from disinterest, but from emotional overload. These behaviors are not disciplinary problems; they are cries for understanding.

That's why grief education and trauma-informed training for teachers is not just helpful—it's essential. Schools should be places of safety and compassion, not sources of further pressure or alienation.

A Final Thought

Grief is tricky. There is no one-size-fits-all response. But with **sensitivity, honesty, and consistent support**, we can help children—both young and old—navigate grief without feeling alone. Whether it's through simple conversations, shared rituals, or offering quiet presence, the way we respond makes all the difference.

Loss is inevitable. But the **way we support each other through it** can shape how deeply we heal.

A Counselor for Grief

People seeking help for grief often don't know where to begin—or what to look for. Grief is overwhelming, disorienting, and deeply personal. That's why it's important to understand what makes grief support effective—and to recognize the difference between **grief counseling** and **grief therapy**. Though these terms are sometimes used interchangeably, they serve distinct purposes and are suited to different types of grieving experiences.

What Is Grief Counseling?

Grief counseling typically begins shortly after a funeral or within the first few weeks following a loved one's passing. Its purpose is to support individuals during the natural grieving process by helping them **adjust to the loss in a healthy and manageable way**. The goal is not to "move on" or "get over it," but to gently guide someone from disoriented or complicated grief into a more **adaptive, integrated experience of grief** over time.

Grief counseling helps individuals:

- Acclimate to life after the loss
- Manage emotional and physical pain
- Overcome psychological or practical obstacles to healing
- Rebuild their lives while forming a new internal relationship with the deceased

Professionals offering grief counseling are typically trained mental health providers—holding at least a **master's degree** in counseling, social work, psychology, or a related field. Ideally, they have completed specialized coursework in grief, loss, and bereavement, as well as internships or supervised experience working with grieving individuals.

It's important to note: a grief counselor does **not** need to have experienced the same type of loss to be effective. While shared experience can foster connection, what truly matters is the counselor's ability to **facilitate healing, foster resilience, and empower clients** through compassion and expertise.

One of the most powerful tools in grief counseling is giving clients space to **tell their grief story**—but only when they're ready. This process should be approached with sensitivity. Counselors may use techniques such as **open-ended questions, reflective listening, gentle encouragement, rephrasing, and validation** to help clients explore their personal understanding of the loss.

A key function of grief counseling is to help clients **actualize the loss**—this may include talking openly about the deceased, revisiting memories, or even visiting a gravesite. Clients are encouraged to identify, name, and process their emotions, and to redirect painful or overwhelming feelings into more constructive outlets. For example, someone experiencing guilt may find healing through:

- Writing a letter to their loved one
- Talking with supportive friends or family
- Expressing themselves through journaling or art

- Processing the emotion in a safe, therapeutic space

What Is Grief Therapy?

Grief therapy is designed for those experiencing **complicated or prolonged grief reactions**—the kind that linger or intensify and begin to interfere with everyday life.

Common forms of complicated grief include:

- **Chronic grief**: persistent, long-term grief that doesn't ease with time
- **Delayed grief**: grief that emerges much later after the loss
- **Masked grief**: grief that presents as physical or emotional symptoms unrelated to the loss
- **Exaggerated grief**: overwhelming or debilitating emotional responses

Grief therapists are often **licensed clinical social workers, psychologists, or professional counselors** with advanced training in trauma, loss, and mental health. They use a wide range of clinical techniques to reduce the **duration, intensity, and impact** of grief-related symptoms.

Therapeutic goals often include:

- Processing complex, unresolved emotions
- Reconstructing a coherent and compassionate narrative of the loss
- Exploring relational wounds or unfinished business
- Supporting long-term adaptation and emotional recovery

Grief therapy also involves ongoing assessment of the client's **emotional, physical, and psychological well-being**, with tailored interventions based on the client's unique needs. Building a strong, trusting therapeutic alliance is a cornerstone of this deeper work.

When to Seek What

In short, both **grief counseling** and **grief therapy** are essential forms of support—but they differ in **depth, scope, and complexity**.

- **Grief counseling** is ideal for those adjusting to a recent loss and seeking guidance through the early stages of grief.
- **Grief therapy** is suited for individuals whose grief is chronic, delayed, overwhelming, or complicated by trauma or unresolved emotional pain.

If you—or someone you care about—is grieving, understanding these distinctions can help ensure you seek the **right kind of support at the right time**. Grief may be universal, but the way we walk through it is deeply personal. Whether you're beginning the journey or feeling stuck somewhere in the middle, know that healing is possible—and help is available.

How to Keep Being a Good Person

I was once asked what I would say to my younger self. This message is for anyone facing difficult circumstances—especially those dealing with challenges involving other people.

Life is a constant battle—externally and internally—and the two are often intertwined. In our personal relationships, professional environments, or social encounters, we face moments that don't go in our favor. Sometimes, the people closest to us weaponize personal information, past mistakes, or our deepest vulnerabilities. These soft spots—our lifelong struggles and emotional wounds—can be easily exploited.

And it doesn't just happen in our private lives. In the workplace, the pressure can be just as intense. Some corporate environments breed competition at the cost of humanity, where coworkers sabotage each other for status, promotions, or favoritism. Sadly, we can have enemies—even when we never asked for them.

There are people, whether in our personal or professional lives, who may actively try to complicate our path. And when that happens, it's easy to mirror the negativity we encounter. We start reflecting the very energy we despise. We hurt others because we were hurt.

This is where the internal and external battles collide.

But here's the truth: **it is essential to maintain a beautiful way of treating yourself and those around you, even when the world feels ugly**. A good heart is a fragile thing—it can be bruised, hardened, and even poisoned by negative experiences. We are always at war within ourselves, trying not to become what we dislike, or worse, what we hate.

Each battle within that war teaches us a vital lesson: **don't let the negativity around you poison you**. And if you already feel poisoned, what you need is medicine—not punishment, not vengeance, but medicine.

That medicine is whatever helps you keep your heart intact. For some, it's found in books like this. For others, it's faith, philosophy, self-help, elders, therapy, journaling, or intentional coping practices. Whatever nourishes your spirit and helps you return to yourself—hold onto it. That's your medicine.

Learning from our experiences is like uncovering treasure in the middle of chaos. It becomes a source of clarity, growth, and inner empowerment. Every painful encounter can be a stepping stone toward a better, more peaceful life—if we allow it.

Sometimes, even ordinary experiences teach powerful lessons. I remember playing pickup basketball games in college—not because I was good, but because I loved the cardio and the fun. I'd often hit the court before lifting weights. Depending on who showed up, the energy shifted. Some players took it seriously—which was their right—but I was there to play casually.

One day, the serious group took things too far. The trash talk turned hostile. Calls became confrontational. Respect disappeared. It wasn't just a game anymore—it became emotionally exhausting, especially since I didn't know anyone personally. But that's what you sometimes agree to when you step onto that court.

The same goes for life. You may step into situations that shift on you—spaces that were once playful but turn hostile without warning. Eventually, you reach a point where you say, "Enough is enough." You realize you don't have to keep showing up to every court, every conflict, or every environment that costs you peace.

So I chose peace. I started playing earlier in the day—or chose the treadmill instead. I adjusted to protect my joy. That small change taught me something big: **you're allowed to change the location, the timing, or the people.**

Sometimes, peace means walking away—even from those you once considered close. But here's the good news: there are incredible people out there who are waiting to be part of your story. The quality of the people you surround yourself with matters deeply.

This is especially true for those who are vulnerable to peer pressure—regardless of age. We must be discerning about who we let into our lives, even if it means creating distance from lifelong friends or even family.

When we recover and protect a good heart, the benefits are endless. We become more connected, more likable, and more at peace. Regret is part of life—but carrying a bitter or negative heart only multiplies that regret. Why? Because we often become what we once promised never to be.

In the end, life's journey is filled with challenges—some external, some internal. And the people we encounter often shape those challenges. Whether in relationships, at work, or in the community, we are constantly tested. But the power to respond with intention always lies within us.

Just as we protect our physical bodies from harm, we must guard our hearts and minds from emotional decay. By choosing to keep a good heart—and seeking the "medicine" of growth through reflection, learning, and connection—we rise above the noise.

The key is knowing when an environment or relationship no longer serves your peace—and having the courage to change it.

Yes, life will bring regrets. But don't let the deepest one be **losing yourself to bitterness**.

True peace is found in discernment, resilience, and choosing what nurtures your soul. Surround yourself with those who uplift and inspire—and you'll not only survive life's battles, but you'll grow stronger through them.

Suffering & Decisions

This section is for those navigating difficult
challenges—whether it's addiction, financial
hardship, health struggles, or the quiet ache of
unfulfilled ambition. It's for anyone who's ever felt
like they're running in place—longing for change,
yet stuck in patterns that sabotage progress.

When I speak of suffering, I don't mean biblical
torment or extreme hardship. I'm not suggesting we
chase discomfort by sleeping on cold floors or
denying ourselves joy. Rather, I'm referring to a
quieter, often ignored kind of suffering—the
emotional unrest that comes from abandoning our
long-term goals for short-term relief. It's the kind of
pain that slowly builds when we give in to what
feels good now but costs us later.

This form of subtle sacrifice—resisting what we
crave—can lead to deeper peace and lasting
fulfillment. That's where delayed gratification
comes in.

Delayed gratification is the intentional act of resisting short-term pleasure in service of long-term purpose. It's turning down instant comforts—junk food, impulsive shopping, toxic relationships—in order to build a life that is rooted in values, meaning, and peace. But let's be honest: this isn't easy. Even when we know better, our desires tug at us. Our wants can become traps—urging us to pursue people, places, and habits that seem comforting but quietly derail our path.

Unchecked desires become distractions. They masquerade as comfort while pulling us further from the life we're truly trying to build.

But we are not powerless. We can reshape our desires. We can train ourselves to find contentment in the present moment, even while striving for something greater. Suffering often arises when we don't get what we want. Like children, even adults can become overwhelmed when desires go unmet. But managing our wants—rather than letting them manage us—is one of the most liberating, empowering paths to peace.

We often reach for what we want as a way to soothe our inner discomfort. But what happens when those comforts aren't available anymore?

Imagine this: What if everything you frequently crave—your favorite foods, your impulse buys, your vacations, or emotionally charged relationships—suddenly became inaccessible?

For some, peace would come from resisting the cookies and choosing vegetables. For others, it might mean breaking the habit of emotional spending that leads to debt. It could mean canceling a trip meant to distract from inner turmoil, or walking away from a relationship that no longer nurtures your growth.

These things may feel good at the moment, but over time, they can pull us off course—drifting further from the peace we say we want.

Life offers us two roads. One is paved with comfort and instant gratification. The other appears more difficult, but leads to true peace. The first is soft underfoot, but lined with invisible thorns. The second may challenge your feet, but it strengthens your soul.

Every day, we're given choices: Do we take the harder road that nurtures our long-term well-being, or do we give in to what feels good now—even if it hurts us later? The temporary sacrifice is what leads to a life of true fulfillment. The key is to consistently choose long-term wellness over momentary relief.

Our decisions shape our destiny. By embracing delayed gratification, we bring ourselves closer to peace—not the fleeting kind, but the kind that endures.

And here's another vital truth: we must keep our end goal in mind. Every small decision either moves us closer or pulls us further away.

If your goal is to save money, even a small, seemingly harmless purchase—a cookie, a shirt, a latte—can quietly undermine your larger vision. If your goal is sobriety, even just one drink can restart a cycle. If your goal is emotional stability, texting that person who triggers your self-doubt could set you back months.

So before we act, we must pause. Reflect. Ask:

- Where does this idea come from?
- What belief is driving this decision?
- Is this truly aligned with the future I want to create?

The more we practice this pause, the stronger we become. The more we choose peace over pleasure, the closer we get to the life we actually want.

Because fulfillment isn't found in what feels good for a moment—it's found in what feels right in the long run.

Coping Mechanisms

Coping mechanisms are essential for maintaining our peace—and for finding our way back to it when we've lost it.

But not all coping mechanisms are created equal. Some, unfortunately, are harmful and detrimental to both mental and physical health. Common examples include smoking, alcohol, drugs, and gambling. These are often the most accessible options because they offer quick relief. But that short-term pleasure often leads to long-term pain.

Many people are never taught how to manage difficult emotions, circumstances, or relationships. As a result, they turn to hedonism—seeking pleasure, pleasure, and more pleasure. The challenge with pleasure is that it's one of the few things in life that seems infinite—you can always crave more, and it's rarely enough.

That's why it becomes crucial to learn positive and sustainable ways to cope—so that life doesn't become an endless cycle of problems followed by self-inflicted wounds that only lead to more suffering.

For me, coping came through a variety of tools—some of which I already had in place. One of the most important has been my practice of ITF Taekwondo, a Korean martial art that I still engage in today.

The physical release of punching, kicking, yelling, and sparring became a profound form of emotional regulation. But martial arts offered more than just a physical outlet—it also provided opportunities for mindful stretching, meditation, discipline, and connection with others facing their own struggles.

Despite the chaos outside, the dojang was a place of stability, growth, and relief from negative thoughts.

Another coping tool that saved me was writing—especially poetry. Through poetry, I could process and untangle what I was feeling, trace its origin, and examine how it affected me. I used literary devices to transform misfortune into art, and I placed those pieces in the books I wrote.

Writing became a way to release mental clutter, to honor the goodness I had experienced, and to grieve what had been lost.

I've also grown comfortable with sitting in stillness—allowing myself to feel deeply. Sometimes that means crying, letting the tears fall without shame. That release, that *"boohoo"* moment, is an act of strength.

It's about building yourself up by facing what hurts—not avoiding it.

And then there's art.

My freestyle art skills aren't anything to brag about—I can color inside the lines, and that's about it. But with guidance, I've been surprised by what I can do. I've come to admire how others turn simple materials into complex expressions. The inner workings of their creativity are astounding, and I hope to explore that more myself.

Art is not only a way to cope—it's also an invitation to explore your interests and discover your capabilities.

That exploration is key. Following your curiosity and investing in your passions can be a powerful part of your coping toolbox.

Whether it's martial arts, writing, art, music, or something else entirely—find what gives you peace, purpose, or perspective.

Build yourself a wall—not to shut the world out, but to block the negativity that tries to invade your mind.

Make that wall strong, resistant, and tall.

Let your coping mechanisms be the bricks.

When Is Your Golden Age?

When people hear the term *"golden age,"* their minds often wander to great civilizations—Mesopotamia, the Roman Empire, the British Empire—or legendary sports teams and Olympic dynasties. These are the eras people look back on with pride, nostalgia, and reverence.

But I believe everyone has their own personal golden era. For some, it's when they were at the top of their academic game—before a traumatic brain injury or psychological hardship altered their path. For others, it was their physical prime—before an accident at work or a sports injury shifted everything.

I once counseled someone who felt deeply broken because their golden age had ended early. They were still young, yet unable to do the things they once loved. Running, walking, skipping, jumping—things that once came effortlessly—were no longer possible. It all changed in a single moment. What took just seconds to unfold ended up reshaping the course of their life. They began to believe there was nothing left worth striving for.

In response, I shared my own story—not to compare, but to show a different way of looking at loss. I've told this story before in other pieces of writing, but each time I share it, there's a new perspective to offer.

I was hit by an SUV. My right leg and left elbow were struck, and I was hospitalized for three days.

- **Day one**: surgery to realign the bones.
- **Day two**: metal plates and pins.

I woke up with my mother by my side. As I groggily came to, I was briefed on what the procedures were and how to manage daily needs—like urinating in a container, with help, because I couldn't move.

The pain was real, and so was the fear. My mom tried to help me sit up, but I yelled at her—not because I didn't love her, but because I was scared. I didn't want to make the wrong move. I didn't want to hurt more than I already did. I felt helpless. And when you feel helpless, sometimes you lash out at the people trying to help.

Then, on the second day, I met a nurse who managed to convince my 11-year-old, prideful self to go to the hospital playroom. It took two nurses and my mother to persuade me, but eventually, I got into the wheelchair and let them roll me in. And what I saw changed me.

There were other kids—some better off, some worse. Children without hair. Children with IVs. Children who were clearly fighting battles much bigger than mine.

That moment taught me something I hadn't seen before: I wasn't alone. I wasn't the only one struggling. We often convince ourselves that no one has it as bad as we do, that we are isolated in our suffering. But that's rarely true.

Connecting with others who are navigating similar pain can be a lifeline. It can help us shift our perspective and realize we are part of something larger than our own pain.

That summer, I took an extended break from school. I had a tutor to help me stay on track, but I couldn't bring myself to let go of my pride and return to school when I was physically able. That decision cost me. I lost my place in the band. The baritone—an instrument I was great at—was taken from me because my grades slipped, and I had to refocus to avoid failing.

As I began walking again, I had to go back for checkups and scans. Eventually, I was told by my doctor that if I were to injure my leg again, I might never walk again. That shook me.

I couldn't walk for three months. Learning how to do it again was grueling—an experience I never want to repeat.

Still, I was young. And like many young people, I wanted to test limits. I joined the high school football team, despite knowing how risky it was.

Leg injuries are common in football. I had seen them firsthand.

Years later, I finally followed through on a long-time idea: joining a martial art. I chose ITF Taekwon-do, of all things—a discipline where kicking is one of the core components.

Today, I still train in it. I love it. And I'm fortunate that I can do it without injury. But not everyone is so lucky.

I share all this to say: sometimes, we lose the things that defined our golden age. And, yes, it hurts to leave those things behind. But we always have the opportunity to begin again.

If one golden era ends, it doesn't mean life has ended. It just means it's time to adapt—and find the next golden age.

It's painful to look back on the past and feel like it's unreachable. But with a shift in perspective, we can look back with gratitude instead of grief. We can choose to honor those moments rather than resent their passing.

Explore new activities. Visit new places. Try new hobbies.

You never know what your next golden age might look like—until you give it the chance to begin.

Why Get Emotional?

Emotions are a tricky thing. They're deeply personal
and unique to each of us, yet universal in their
presence. We all experience loss, disappointment,
grief, or anger—but how we handle those emotions
can drastically shape the outcomes in our lives.

I've had moments when regulating my emotions
was incredibly difficult. One of those times came
with the loss of a relationship—due in part to my
inability to manage criticism, judgment, and conflict
effectively. There were no clear boundaries, no
solution-focused approach. I take accountability for
not managing my emotions better, which led to
saying and doing things that harmed the connection.
That experience taught me that emotional
mismanagement often leads to regret and loss.

If you want to preserve what matters most in your
life—relationships, peace of mind, personal
growth—emotional regulation is essential. We're
constantly tested, especially in leadership or
high-stress environments.

For instance, when I lead group discussions, I often encounter individuals who dominate the space, taking long detours before making a point. In those moments, I maintain poise, gently interject, validate their contribution, and guide the conversation forward with respect and purpose.

But not every challenge is so subtle. One time, during a group session, someone directed a hostile, passive-aggressive comment at me in front of everyone. Looking directly at me, they said, "I ought to smack him—with that tone of voice and cutting me off. But ya know, I don't do that anymore."

I smiled and replied calmly, "Thank you for sharing." And I moved on.

You don't have to fight fire with fire. Sometimes, you fight fire with water—with composure, grace, and discipline.

My ability to maintain emotional composure has been shaped by my involvement in public speaking and martial arts. Whether it's speaking in front of a large crowd or stepping into the ring against someone who wants to defeat you, these experiences pressure you in ways few others can. You learn to stay calm under fire. You gain perspective. You become mentally tough.

That mental toughness extends into other areas. Dance, sports, competitions, performances—these all teach us how to navigate fear and emotional intensity. The goal is to align yourself with positivity, growth, and composure, rather than let frustration or sadness dictate your actions.

Holding onto negative emotions only hurts you. In one of the men's groups I lead, I told the members: "We have to choose how we're going to feel today." That's a powerful statement. Emotions are a choice—one we make every day.

Start your morning by acknowledging your power to shape the tone of your day, regardless of external circumstances. Yes, some things are hard—like grief, breakups, or rejection—but starting with intention makes a difference.

In my Taekwon-do classes, we have a tradition: When asked how we're doing, we respond with "Fantastic!"—even if it's not true. It sets a tone, and even a small shift in language can create a shift in mindset.

You might not always feel fantastic, but sometimes, you have to fake it till you make it. That doesn't mean suppressing pain—it means doing the internal work to heal while projecting the confidence and positivity you want to embody.

When you step into uncomfortable situations—like trying something new and failing in front of others—don't quit. Others are more focused on themselves than you realize. Embrace the discomfort. That's how growth happens.

In my emotion regulation workshops, I share tools like meditation, journaling, drawing, walking, and positive affirmations. We explore the power of choosing peace, creating emotionally supportive environments, and avoiding emotional triggers. A candle, a song, a walk outside, a favorite scent—these small things can lift your spirit and restore your balance.

Equally important is expressing how you feel. Bottled-up emotions find their way out—often at the worst times. Let it out in healthy, intentional ways. Write it. Speak it. Move it out of your body.

Lastly, consider how appearance affects emotion. I learned this during an internship where I dressed too casually at first. After being called out, I changed my wardrobe—choosing business casual and experimenting with style, color, and image. The change was dramatic. People treated me with more respect, opened doors (literally and figuratively), and gave me space to lead.

The way you dress influences how others see you—and how you see yourself. Confidence, courage, and dignity are key to emotional health.

So take time. Dress well. Be bold. Find your style. Be authentically you.

Even on the hard days, show up as the person you're becoming. Because eventually, with enough consistency and heart, you'll see those changes reflected back at you—in your life, your relationships, and your peace of mind.

How to Boost Self-Esteem

Self-esteem is not a fixed trait—it's an evolving process that shifts with time, experience, and growth. What we think about ourselves is often distorted—shaped by past experiences, societal standards, and internalized doubt.

But here's the truth: self-esteem is defined not by what we can't change, but by how we choose to live with—and respond to—what we can. Whatever you can't change, learn to live with it—not in defeat, but in peace. And whatever you can change, approach it with compassion and purpose.

Sometimes, you have to get a little delusional—in the best way possible. Start speaking life into yourself until the positive beliefs become your reality. Train your mind to think positively about your image—mentally, physically, and emotionally. Use creative expression as a tool for transformation. Talk to yourself out loud, write in a journal, sing your truth, draw your emotions, or write poems and stories.

These outlets can help you access the deeper layers of insecurity that quietly erode your self-esteem. Once you uncover those insecurities, self-examination becomes crucial. Reflect deeply: What triggered these negative thought patterns? Why do they keep showing up? Then, prepare to go to war with them—not with anger, but with intention. Replace old narratives with empowering truths. Laugh at the outdated thoughts that once held you back. Ask yourself: Why am I choosing to stay small? What is the real benefit of tearing myself down?

Easier said than done—I know. But life is too short to stay shackled to self-hate. We all have aspects of ourselves we wish were different. Some things we love about ourselves go unnoticed by others. You might receive compliments one day and feel invisible the next. Some people adore your character; others might be turned off by it. One day, a dog might jump for joy at your presence, while a rabbit bolts at the sight of you.

The point is this: other people's perceptions do not define you. They don't determine your worth or what you should love about yourself.

It took me a while to realize that much of what bothers us about ourselves doesn't originate from within. It's absorbed from the world around us—social media, comparisons, criticism, conditioning. Be mindful of what you allow into your mental space. What you consume shapes your beliefs, your self-image, and how you treat both yourself and others.

As we grow on this journey of self-esteem and self-love, we often don't realize we're already ahead. I remember my graduate professor once saying, "Sometimes your community just hasn't caught up to where you are." That hit hard.

We forget our talents, our values, the unique energy we bring to the table. For example, I found martial arts—not by thinking about it, but by doing it. I became good at it. Passionate. Proficient. It's now part of my identity and a huge boost to my self-esteem. I also surprised myself in a painting class. With a little guidance, I discovered that I'm more creative than I thought. Something I used to admire from a distance is now a part of my own story. That shift opened me to new capabilities and expanded my self-perception even further.

Sometimes, we wrongly reduce self-esteem to physical appearance or material achievements. But we're so much more than that. We often overlook the strengths that truly set us apart—courage, character, compassion, resilience. Don't let these invisible victories go unrecognized.

Another important piece of this journey is prioritizing yourself. Helping others is noble, but constantly pouring into others without filling your own cup leads to emotional burnout. You must honor your goals, protect your peace, and stand firm in your boundaries.

This isn't selfish—it's sustainable. Balancing self-care with care for others is challenging, but necessary. You can't pour from an empty cup. Your well-being matters just as much as anyone else's, and preserving your mental and emotional energy allows you to give from a place of strength rather than sacrifice.

So, remember: self-esteem starts with honesty, grows with self-reflection, and thrives through bold action. Speak kindly to yourself. Discover new talents. Set firm boundaries. And above all, never forget: you are allowed to love yourself fiercely, even while you're still becoming who you want to be.

What Unresolved Conflict Can Do

Conflict has existed since the dawn of time—regardless of what you believe in. It's part of the human experience, and no matter how advanced we become, it won't disappear. But the goal isn't to eliminate conflict altogether. It's to **understand it, to manage it**, and most importantly, to **adjust ourselves in ways that preserve peace**.

Sometimes, peace arrives after the storm. Other times, the storm can be diverted entirely. And in some cases, the storm overstays its welcome, lasting far longer than it should.

When conflict remains unresolved, it rarely stays contained. It leaves residue. That residue becomes emotional weight—resentment, frustration, bitterness—that people carry long after the original moment has passed. This burden doesn't just shape how they view the person they conflicted with—it can alter how they see **everyone and everything**.

Unresolved Conflict and the Lens of Life

When we don't actively process conflict, we begin to **generalize**. We paint people and situations with the same brush—whether they deserve it or not. Without self-awareness and emotional tools, conflict can harden us. We start expecting the worst. We become defensive. We misread intentions and jump to conclusions, even with those who had nothing to do with our pain.

To illustrate this, I'll share something simple, even silly—but surprisingly revealing.

When I was young, I lost a tooth by biting into a pear. Without much logic at the time, I associated that pain with pears in general. I stopped eating them. I avoided them. Just the sight of a pear reminded me of the discomfort I felt. My mind made a shortcut: *pears = pain.*

Looking back, I realize how irrational that was. But that's exactly what unresolved conflict does—it

builds irrational associations between experiences and expectations.

Now think: How often do we treat people like pears?

How many of us associate an entire person, group, or setting with a past hurt that may no longer apply? When certain names come up, when familiar faces reappear, our body may react with tension. We might feel anger, dread, or anxiety—without even consciously understanding why. We slip into **fight-or-flight**, not from present danger, but from past memory.

A Real-Life Example

Here's a more grounded story. I once went to a birthday dinner with my family. It was a great night—laughter, good food, and celebration. But when the check came, things changed. The restaurant required the bill to be paid as one group, not individually. People contributed what they owed for their own meals, but somehow, there was still $100–300 unaccounted for—mainly due to gratuity and overlooked items like desserts.

Tension rose. Arguments sparked. Some felt embarrassed, others defensive. I personally felt a chain of emotions: discomfort, frustration, and eventually, avoidance. From that moment on, I found myself **hesitating to eat in large groups**. I developed the perception that people couldn't be trusted to hold their financial weight—and that perception began shaping how I interacted in social settings.

It was one experience. But it had ripple effects. It adjusted how I viewed people, especially in group situations—regardless of who they were. That's the danger of unprocessed conflict: it can subtly damage **even the relationships we value most**. It creates friction where there was once ease. Distance where there was once closeness.

Reflection: What Are You Still Carrying?

Conflict, when left unchecked, **reshapes our worldview**. It can turn optimism into suspicion, compassion into defensiveness, and peace into tension. We begin living in emotional armor—guarding ourselves from imagined threats born from real memories.

So, here's the challenge: **Think about the "pears" in your life.**

- What past conflicts have you carried into present relationships?
- What settings make you uncomfortable, and why?
- Have you been painting new people with old brushes?

Your experiences are valid. The feelings are real. But they don't have to dictate your future interactions. Healing begins with awareness. Peace begins when we acknowledge that the past doesn't have to poison the present.

In closing: Conflict is part of life—but carrying it forever doesn't have to be. Learn to recognize when the storm has passed. Learn to put the burden down.

Your peace—and your relationships—are worth it.

Conflict to Clarity

Conflict, whether mild or intense, leaves an imprint. As explored in the previous essay, when left unaddressed, it shapes how we see people, places, and even ourselves. We carry that emotional residue into new interactions—often unaware that we're reacting not to the moment, but to our memory of pain. So how do we move forward? How do we stop conflict from stealing our peace and tainting our outlook?

The answer lies not in avoidance, but in **resolution and restoration**.

Conflict is natural. But staying stuck in it is not. What matters most is how we respond to the aftermath: whether we allow conflict to create distance and resentment, or we use it to build bridges, deepen understanding, and foster emotional maturity.

Here's how.

---

1. Identify the Source of the Residue

The first step toward healing is honest **awareness**.
If we don't name what hurt us, we can't begin to
heal from it.

Ask yourself:

- *What specific moment or interaction keeps
  replaying in my head?*
- *Who was involved, and what did I feel at the
  time?*
- *What did I need in that moment that I didn't
  receive: validation, an apology, respect,
  fairness?*

Often, our reactions in the present are tied to
unresolved feelings in the past. Identifying that
source helps separate the past from the present. You
begin to see the "pear" for what it is—not the object
of pain, but the trigger of an older wound.

Action Step: Journal for 10–15 minutes about a
lingering conflict or negative association. Focus not

just on what happened, but how it made you feel—and how that feeling has followed you.

---

2. Practice Reframing, Not Repressing

Healing is not about pretending things didn't hurt. It's about *reframing* the story so that it empowers rather than paralyzes.

Reframing means:

- Acknowledging the hurt **without letting it define you**
- Choosing to see the situation as a lesson, not a curse
- Focusing on what the experience taught you about people, boundaries, or yourself

For example, instead of thinking, *"People can't be trusted in group settings,"* try: *"I value shared responsibility, so in the future, I'll express expectations clearly or choose settings where that's respected."*

This small shift protects your peace and restores your agency.

Action Step: Rewrite a memory of conflict from the perspective of what you learned. Then, write down one boundary or behavior you'll use to protect yourself without closing off from others.

---

3. Have the Courageous Conversation

If it's safe and appropriate, sometimes the path to resolution is direct communication. A single honest conversation can dissolve years of resentment. Not all conflict deserves a response—but **some relationships deserve a second chance**.

Before reaching out:

- Reflect: *Is this person willing or capable of mutual understanding?*
- Clarify your goal: *Do I want reconciliation, clarity, or simply to express how I felt?*

- Prepare your words: Focus on "I" statements, not accusations. (*"I felt unseen when..." vs. "You never..."*)

If the conversation doesn't go how you hoped, remember: *Healing isn't dependent on their reaction. It's dependent on your release.*

Action Step: Write a "letter you may or may not send." Express all the emotions you're holding in. Then decide: Will you send it? Or simply let it go?

---

4. Develop a Reset Ritual for Emotional Recovery

In times of stress or conflict, we often spiral. A reset ritual is a personal practice that brings you back to center—calming your body and clarifying your mind.

Examples include:

- Taking a mindful walk, focusing on your breath and surroundings

- Creating a calming playlist and listening while journaling
- Practicing a short breathing exercise or guided meditation
- Physical movement: martial arts, yoga, dance—release helps process

Reset rituals allow us to process emotion without dumping it on others or bottling it up. These rituals create space between feeling and reaction.

Action Step: Identify 1–2 activities that bring you peace. Next time you're triggered by a past wound, *pause and practice your reset ritual before responding.*

---

5. Stop Generalizing and Start Individualizing

Just because one experience hurt you doesn't mean every similar one will. Generalizing keeps us guarded, even when the threat is gone.

Individualizing means:

- Giving people a clean slate—even if they resemble someone who hurt you
- Evaluating situations based on **what's actually happening**, not your past fears
- Catching yourself when you use words like "always," "never," or "they all"

Every person and situation is unique. If you lump them all together, you rob yourself of new, healthy connections.

Action Step: The next time you catch yourself generalizing, pause and ask: *"Is this person responsible for my past pain—or am I projecting?"*

---

6. Strengthen Your Emotional Immune System

Just like we care for our physical health, we must care for our emotional resilience.

You do this by:

- **Daily self-check-ins**: "How am I really feeling today?"
- **Setting healthy boundaries**: Say no when your peace is at risk
- **Being around emotionally mature people** who model calm communication
- **Limiting exposure to toxic environments** (online and offline)

The more you train your emotional awareness, the less likely you are to carry unprocessed conflict. You'll begin to notice pain earlier—and process it faster.

Action Step: Create a weekly check-in list:

- What drained me this week?
- What nourished me?
- What do I need to feel restored?

7. Forgive—Even if They Don't Deserve It

This is the hardest part. But it's often the most freeing.

Forgiveness isn't about approving what happened. It's about *refusing to let it poison your life any longer*. It's for **you**, not them.

You can forgive someone:

- Without ever speaking to them again
- Without receiving an apology
- Without forgetting what happened

Forgiveness says: *"This pain doesn't own me anymore. I deserve to feel free again."*

Action Step: Write down the name of someone you're ready to release. Say out loud: *"I release the hold this memory has over me. I choose peace over poison."* Burn or rip the paper as a symbolic act of release.

8. Live Forward, Not Backward

The past deserves reflection—but not obsession.
Once you've done the inner work, make the
conscious choice to *live forward.*

That means:

- Creating new positive experiences to
  override old ones
- Showing up to events you once avoided
- Trusting people again—slowly, wisely, but
  genuinely
- Letting joy and curiosity replace fear

Each time you engage with the world in a way that
contradicts your pain, you reclaim power, you
redefine what's possible.

Action Step: Schedule one activity this month that
you once avoided due to past conflict. Go in with
new energy, a clear boundary, and an open mind.

Final Reflection: Let Your Peace Be Loud

Peace doesn't mean life is quiet. It means your heart is clear. It means your mind is no longer on edge. Conflict will always exist—but *how you hold it makes all the difference.*

The burden doesn't have to be permanent.

You don't have to carry "pears" from 10 years ago.

You don't have to see every group gathering as a threat.

You don't have to live in fear of repetition.

You get to decide who you become after conflict. You get to choose peace, clarity, connection, and growth.

And when you do, you model to others that healing is not only possible—it's powerful.

Testimonials

JG
I loved the interview on *WBFO What's Next*
today. I could sense your genuine nature, humility,
and wisdom—that's why I wanted to connect.
Thank you!

JC:
It has been a true pleasure watching Dorian
Withrow grow into the leader he is today. I first met
Dorian through the *Breaking Barriers Youth
Leadership Council*, where he stood out as a
thoughtful, driven, and dependable young man.
Over time, I watched him transform from a
participant into a mentor, pouring into others with
the same care and intention that had been shown to
him. His journey has been nothing short of
inspiring, and I was incredibly proud when he
became a published author, using his voice to uplift
and empower others. Dorian exemplifies what it
means to lead with purpose, and I have no doubt
that he will continue to make a meaningful impact
wherever he goes.

JE:
I've known Dorian Withrow Jr. for the past four and
a half years, and it has been my pleasure and honor!
His tenacity for greatness speaks volumes. He
carries himself with deep respect and humility,

staying true to his vision while creating his legacy. His work as an author is both inspiring and motivating. His growth and development as an individual have been tremendous, and I look forward to seeing him continue to flourish and prosper in the future!

C:
I have known Dorian Withrow for over five years, and in that time, I've seen him grow tremendously as a martial artist. He is an excellent student who consistently pushes himself to improve. He's also a great competitor—focused, disciplined, and always striving to perform at his best while maintaining a respectful and sportsmanlike attitude. Dorian is incredibly talented yet remains humble. He genuinely cares about those around him, which is especially evident in the thoughtful support and guidance he offers during partner work. He always greets everyone with a smile. His dedication, work ethic, and friendly attitude make him a valuable part of our school.

S.C:
Hi, Mr. Withrow, my dear! I really enjoyed this interview. I feel like this is a topic that rarely gets discussed, yet it is so needed—especially in the Black community. Years ago, an old friend told me that mental health is often unacknowledged in the

Black community, and I still believe that to be true. From a personal standpoint, I can relate to traumatic experiences and mental health struggles. I'm still working on my healing journey.

I'm so happy for you, Mr. Withrow. I truly enjoyed this interview. Thank you for sharing it with me! I hope to hear from you soon. Stay safe, and God bless you, my dear! More people need to know that they are not alone in this journey.

FM:
When I first met Dorian, he was a preteen—no more than 11 or 12 years old—through my work at the *Boys & Girls Clubs of Buffalo* as a youth development professional. He was a quiet, timid young man, which may have drawn me toward him. In many ways, he reminded me of myself, but he also had an intellect beyond his years. Every year, the BGC hosts an event for young leaders in WNY and surrounding areas called *Youth of the Year*. It took some convincing, but with the help of a few colleagues, we encouraged Dorian to participate. He placed second in our region, but honestly, he has only soared higher ever since. He graduated high school with multiple honors and scholarships and did the same at Canisius College. Dorian is truly a success story. He has published multiple books, regularly serves as a keynote speaker at various

events, and he hasn't even hit his ceiling yet.
Whoever said "the sky's the limit" was talking
about my boy, my friend, my family—Dorian
Withrow Jr.

Sincerely,
A proud friend and mentor

T:
Dorian, our resident poet. I loved having you in the
group, and I'm always excited when you speak.
Thank you for your humor and perspective.

R:
You brought such a fun vibe and energy to this
group. Your attention to detail and comprehension
of others' experiences is truly admirable. You have
such a cool presence!

L:
Dorian, you had such a meaningful presence in our
group. Your calm and kind demeanor makes you a
natural counselor. Thank you for the comment/gift
about my siblings—that meant a lot to me.

A:
Dorian, your insight in the group was amazing and
creative! You truly have a way with words. I can't

wait to see the beautiful things you'll write about in the future!

PL:
I can't wait to hear about all the wonderful things you'll accomplish. New York Times Bestselling Author—I see it already!

K:
Thanks for being such a cool and creative presence in our group. I appreciate your support when we were partnered up together. I shared vulnerable things, and you made me feel heard and seen. Those are incredible qualities for a counselor.

J:
You have such a creative mind! I loved how you led our group sessions. I wish you the best of success—I know you will achieve great things!

C:
Thank you for always being willing to share your opinion and perspective. I appreciate how thoughtful and insightful you are in your responses. You are a great group leader—stay happy and healthy!

Dr. C.S. Jr.

Every so often, I have the absolute privilege of meeting someone who truly inspires and motivates me. Even more rarely, that person is someone so young. Upon meeting Dorian Withrow Jr., I immediately recognized that he was wise beyond his years. His business acumen, writing ability, speaking prowess, and affable personality make him a serious contender for greatness in whatever path he chooses to pursue. I have invited Dorian to speak as a motivational guest for my human services students at SUNY Erie Community College, and he never fails to bring out something in them that inspires self-improvement. He has a unique ability to connect with people in a way that sets him apart from other speakers. If I had been half as focused as he is at his age, there's no telling where I might be today.

T. O'-W:
Although he is quite soft-spoken, Dorian Withrow Jr.'s words carry a great deal of weight. I first met Dorian in passing during a meeting for the Boys and Young Men of Color and Breaking Barriers group. The second time I encountered him was at a weekend camping experience with the same group, down in Holland, New York. That morning, Dorian led all of us—adults, young men, and boys—in a workout session that included pushups, planks, and

more. Needless to say, many of us were exhausted before the day had even begun. Since that weekend, in my former role as a public media journalist, I've had the opportunity to interview Dorian on a daily show I hosted for two years. It was through that medium that I got to know him much better. He's an author, a martial arts instructor, and, in my opinion, an all-around solid human being. Dorian's soft-spokenness belies a powerful drive to help others—whether through writing, martial arts, or mentorship.

Master Ab:

I am thrilled to write this testimonial for my fellow martial artist and Black Belt, Mr. Withrow, whose journey as a writer has been nothing short of inspiring. What I admire most about Mr. Withrow is his commitment to making literature that is accessible and impactful. He has dedicated himself to creating works that help others overcome barriers in personal growth, foster peaceful living, and build better relationships. His unique approach to writing—encompassing poetry, short stories, and educational content—demonstrates his versatility and creativity. Each piece he crafts carries a distinctive voice, whether it be through heartfelt poetry, engaging dialogue, or insightful essays. Mr. Withrow's dedication to his craft and his desire to make a positive impact on society truly set him apart as a writer. I wholeheartedly encourage anyone to explore his work, as it not only reflects his passion but also offers valuable insights for personal development. I am proud to support Mr. Withrow on this incredible journey and can't wait to see where his talent takes him next!

About the Author

Dorian Scott Withrow Jr. was born on April 13, 2000, in Buffalo, New York. He completed most of his education through the Amherst Central School District. Dorian began to flourish in high school, overcoming numerous challenges and achieving success through his involvement in several programs, including Youth of the Year, Jack and Jill of America, Leadership Buffalo, and Breaking Barriers. In 2018, he was accepted into Canisius University, where he majored in Animal Behavior, Ecology, and Conservation (ABEC) and minored in Philosophy. During his time at university, Dorian remained active in Breaking Barriers, attending meetings, engaging in activism, and participating in podcast projects. He also developed a new passion: ITF Taekwondo. Dorian graduated from Canisius University in May 2022 with a Bachelor of Science. He went on to earn his Master's degree in Mental Health Counseling from the University at Buffalo, graduating in May 2025.

This achievement reflects his ongoing dedication to supporting others and promoting mental wellness.

Youth of the Year (Boys and Girls Club)

Youth of the Year is a prestigious achievement awarded to members of the Boys and Girls Clubs for their community involvement, leadership, character, and mentorship of younger peers. Recipients of this honor not only gain recognition but also have the opportunity to advance to higher levels of competition and personal development. Selected youth from various Boys and Girls Clubs across the city participate in workshops to prepare for the next stage. These workshops cover public speaking, writing, teaching, and more. Although Dorian did not advance to the next stage, he placed second out of six competitors—a notable accomplishment.

Jack & Jill Of America

Dorian was also involved in Jack & Jill of America, a program designed for young Black males. The program offered various workshops focused on leadership, fitness, dressing to impress, public speaking, and dance (including West African and Urban Ballroom styles). It fostered a strong network among its members and emphasized the importance of community service, providing exposure to a diverse group of individuals and contributing to Dorian's personal and character development. The program culminated in an African rite of passage, symbolizing the transition from boyhood to manhood. The final ceremony included speeches, dance performances, and the rite of passage ritual. As part of the tradition, each participant chose a name to represent their new identity. Dorian chose the name *Adwin*, meaning "thinker and artist."

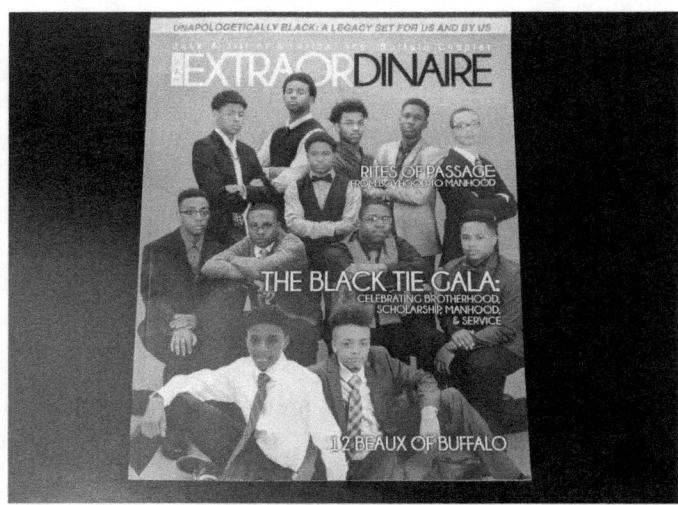

Leadership Buffalo

Dorian participated in Leadership Buffalo during his first retreat, where he met many fascinating individuals from diverse backgrounds. The program offered a variety of workshops focused on leadership, cooking, dining etiquette (including a lesson from a former butler to the Queen of England), diversity, inclusion, and more. It was an incredible opportunity for teamwork and for building meaningful connections.

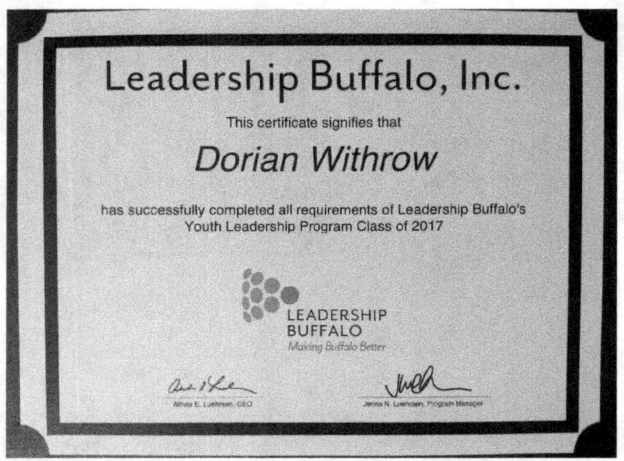

Honors and Rewards

Dorian received numerous honors and awards in high school. He was inducted into the National Honor Society for maintaining merit roll status and also attended Harkness Erie 1 BOCES for Animal Science, where he earned membership in the National Technical Honor Society. Additionally, he received scholarships from the Buffalo Urban League and Delta Sigma Theta Sorority. Dorian graduated from high school in 2018 and went on to pursue a Bachelor of Science degree at Canisius University. He is now a proud alumnus. During his academic journey, Dorian developed a strong passion for philosophy, which led to his induction into Phi Sigma Tau, the international honor society for philosophy. He was also awarded the St. Thomas Aquinas Award in Philosophy in recognition of his exceptional academic achievements in the field. Moreover, Dorian was honored with the Martin Luther King Award for his commitment to promoting social justice, social harmony, civil rights, human rights, advocacy for

the poor, and non-violence. He is a graduate and
ongoing youth council member of Breaking
Barriers, a program for males of color ages 12 to 24
that focuses on policy advocacy, mentoring,
leadership, and improving educational and
employment opportunities. Through this program,
Dorian gained invaluable knowledge and formed
meaningful connections. He has also become a
social justice trainer and continues to contribute to
the Breaking Barriers podcast series.

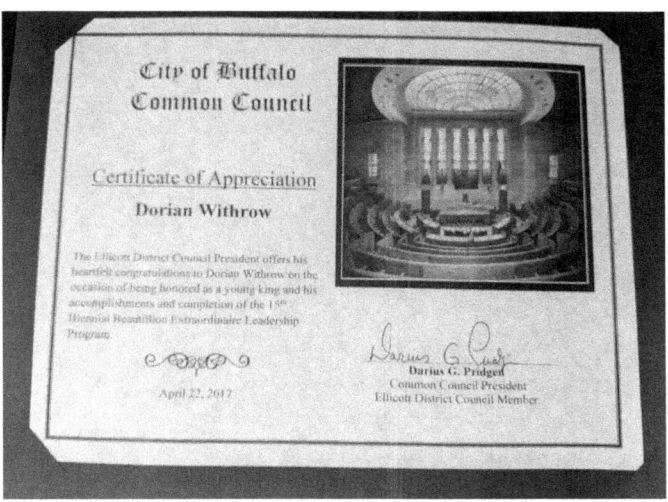

ITF Taekwondo

Dorian is also a martial artist and an ITF
Taekwondo practitioner. He has some foundational
knowledge of Isshin Ryu Karate, passed down from
his grandfather. Dorian began training in ITF
Taekwondo in May 2019. Through diligent and
persistent effort, he earned affiliation with the
Master's Club. He is also a member of the
D.E.L.T.A. Team (Dedicated, Enthusiastic, Loyal,
Teaching Assistant), where he helps teach and
positively impact the lives of others. Dorian has
progressed from Il-Dan (first-degree black belt) to
Ee-Dan (second-degree black belt) and remains
passionate about continuing his training and growth
in the art.

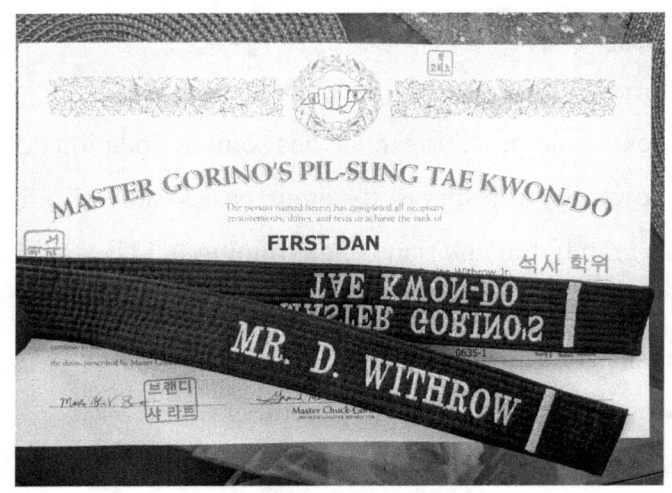

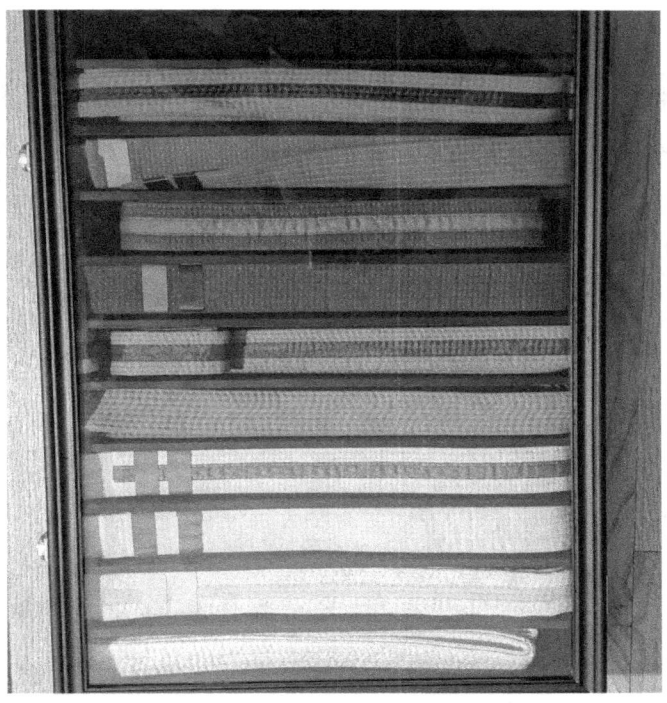

Books Authored By Dorian S. Withrow Jr.

Book Alphabetical

Speak! Young Brown People, Speak. We are listening!
A.L. Savvy Publications 2014, 2022

Thoughts Of Creativity King 114 Realities. Dorian
Withrow Jr., Withrow LLC, Buffalo NY, 2022

Wisdom 45 Advice. Dorian S. Withrow Jr., Withrow
LLC, Buffalo NY, 2022

Conversations You Need. Dorian Withrow Jr., Withrow
LLC, Buffalo NY, 2023

Don't Be A Cactus: How to Make Connections &
Resolve Conflicts. Dorian Withrow Jr., Withrow LLC,
Buffalo NY, 2024